THE DOLPHINS' GIFT

Elizabeth Gawain

WHATEVER
PUBLISHING

© 1981 Elizabeth Gawain

Published by Whatever Publishing
158 E. Blithedale, Suite 4
Mill Valley, California 94941

Cover, book design and technical drawings by Julio Lynch
Other artwork by David Fairchild
Photo credits, see page 248

LC Card Number 81-3039

ISBN 0-931432-10-3

Manufactured in the United States of America

Table of Contents

Chapters:

To dolphins swimming free in the sea
who come to seek our touch
And to humans who respond
openly and naturally
to such offers of friendship
This book is dedicated

1

Dolphins Seeking Us

How would you like to stay at a beach where dolphins come in from the sea to play? Where, if you should wade into the calm water, two or three dolphins would glide up to your knees, look into your eyes making little sounds, and allow you to stroke their sides as they swim past you? "Hello, Nick," you say to one, dangling a fish by its tail. He takes the fish and swallows it with that mischievous dolphin grin. As he glides away he tilts to one side so that one eye is out of the water looking at you. Gazing into that eye you feel a strong sense of belonging, of freedom and peace. Does it sound like a dream? It was a dream come true for me.

There is a remote beach in western Australia where a whole family of wild dolphins (or we prefer to say "free" dolphins, that have never been captured or trained) have been coming in to the beach from the open sea every day for many years to visit the people there. The couple who

own the fishing camp at this beach have given names to
about a dozen of these animals, and anyone who visits
there can easily learn to recognize several of them, call
them by name, pet them, and hand them a fish to eat. The
dolphins come every day for three-quarters of the year to
greet the people, play around for a few hours, then swim
away again far out of sight in the open sea, to come again
the next day. Even during the very hot season, when they
do not appear daily, they come once every week or so.

No one has ever attempted to restrain them or to
interfere with them in any way, and the couple who own
the camp are determined that no one ever shall. But anyone is welcome to stand in the water and visit with the
dolphins, and it is a wonderful experience to do so. They
are especially fond of children, and we can hope that the
many youngsters who come each year and learn to love a
free dolphin will carry in their hearts always a determination to keep these beautiful intelligent creatures free and
safe throughout the world.

Why do these dolphins come to this particular beach
regularly and make friends with anyone who will take the
trouble to wade into the water? Some believe that they
have a message for us, if we can learn to understand.
Perhaps by reading about them you can discover what the
message might be for you.

There are many instances throughout history of a
dolphin befriending a human, and even some instances of
a dolphin coming in to a shore regularly to see the people
there, or of a dolphin meeting boats or a diver regularly in a
particular area in the sea or a bay. But according to a
number of reliable organizations who take an interest in
such things, this is the only instance ever reported of a
whole group of wild dolphins who, on their own initiative,
come regularly to the same beach, and right into shallow
water, seeking to be touched. There are many other remarkable aspects of this case of dolphin contact with
humans, but we shall go into those details later. First let us
trace the history of how it all began.

On the west coast of Australia is Shark Bay, perhaps 50 miles across and 80 miles indented from the coast, with the Peron Peninsula dividing the large bay roughly in half. The bay opens to the northwest. In the early days of the English presence in Australia, a seagoing vessel named "Monkey" was sent to Shark Bay to search for another ship that had been lost, and the Monkey spent some time at a spot on the east coast of the central peninsula. The spot became known by the strange name of "Monkey Mia" (pronounced "my-ah"). "Mia" is the Australian aborigines' word for "home," so Monkey Mia means "home of the Monkey," the port of the vessel Monkey. The Monkey had on board the surveyors who first examined this area, and they referred to the place as Monkey Mia in their journals.

It is called "Monkey My-ah," aboriginal "home" of the vessel "Monkey."

Then about 100 years ago there was at this same spot a
pearling community of Chinese people, employed by an
English commercial venture, and that was also known as
Monkey Mia. (There are still pearl oysters in the bay, and
occasionally someone finds a lovely pearl in an oyster
shell idly picked up on the beach.)

By 1900, on the west coast of the peninsula, opposite
Monkey Mia, the town of Denham was an established
community and a growing commercial fishing port.
Ocean-going vessels called there, and sometimes would
seek shelter there from a storm, on their way from England
to the cities of Australia. The track across the peninsula
from Denham to the old pearl fishing site was still used
occasionally, and maps continued to show the trail and to
label the place Monkey Mia. Long after the pearl fishing
industry ended, the site of the old Chinese community
was used as a little camp for fishing. Right into the 1970's
the place was visited by recreation fishermen who would
come and camp for a week or a month to enjoy the rich
catches of fish in the bay. It is still frequented today, and
still called Monkey Mia.

We do not know of any contact between the Chinese
pearl fishers and any dolphins that may have been around
at that time, nor indeed of contact between dolphins and
any aborigines that may have ever lived on the peninsula
(although that would be interesting to investigate).

Recently, for more than 25 years now, there have been
stories of very friendly dolphins around Monkey Mia, and
the first dolphin we know of to be given a name came in
the 1950's. It seems that it was the custom, as it is even
now, for the fishermen to catch a large number of small
fish in the early morning to be used for the day's bait.
There was a particular dolphin who took an interest in the
success of the bait catch, and developed the habit of round-
ing up schools of small fish and herding them towards the
humans! Dolphins are fairly well known to do similar
helpful things for man for no apparent gain to themselves.
It seems to be a situation of — "Well, what else is there to

do? You want to play a game of catching fish? All right, I can find you plenty of fish."

It became a regular occurrence. They say that every morning, at exactly the same time (7:15, according to my source), Old Charley, as the dolphin can came to be called, would appear and herd schools of bony herring towards the fishermen. He would continue to do this for an hour or more as the men hauled in their fish, but then at 8:30 he would scatter the fish, as if to say, "That's your share for today."

There are many tales of Old Charley and his games with the fishermen, which all add up to about what I have related, with possibly some embellishments of the sort fishermen are famous for. But one thing is certain — that a particular dolphin made frequent gestures of interest in the activities of human beings over a period of a number of years, so that many different persons recognized him and felt kindly disposed towards him. It may be that some fishermen did *not* feel so friendly towards him, however, thinking perhaps that dolphins were eating the fish that *they* might catch if the dolphins were not there. In any case, a dolphin was found dead on the beach one day and was identified as Old Charley. Apparently the identification was correct, because Old Charley never appeared in the bay again to round up schools of bony herring for the fishermen. Some say the dead dolphin had been shot, but this has not been documented, and it is possible that it was a natural death. We know only that a dolphin body was found, and that Charley was not seen again.

The exact dates of these events are difficult to determine, but apparently other dolphins had become quite friendly even during the time that Old Charley was doing his helpful act. At least by the early 1960's, when the fishermen tended to bring their whole families to camp by the beach at Monkey Mia, there were a number of dolphins that would linger around the long wooden jetty, and around the small boats that came and went, and it was customary to throw an occasional small fish to the attentive animals. It is very probable that this had gone on for many years, so that the dolphins came to regard the humans as pleasant neighbors who played a fun game.

There is no reason at all to assume that the dolphins needed the fish that were thrown to them by the fishing people. The bony herring and yellowtails that make up their favorite fare are plentiful in the bay, and a healthy dolphin is at least as expert at catching them as are the human beings. It seems extremely probable, then as now, that they simply enjoy the game.

There is a letter in the file at Monkey Mia from a woman who says that, some years ago when she was a teenage girl on holiday with her family at the fishing camp, she was the one who first enticed the dolphins to take a fish from her hand. According to her letter, this would have been around 1964. By this time the dolphins had become accustomed to come quite close to someone in a boat or on the jetty, or to someone standing in the shallow water at the beach, in order to be thrown a fish from close range. This young girl worked at getting the dolphins to come closer and closer before giving up the fish, until she had them literally eating out of her hand. They have been doing it ever since.

The next dolphin to be called by name was Old Speckledy Belly. She had markings similar to big brown freckles on her pale belly, and they say she was almost toothless, with her wrinkled mouth sunken in as an old woman's mouth would be if she had no teeth. This dolphin became very tame indeed. She would come into the shallow water to take a fish from the hand of anyone who offered it, even if she had never seen the person before, and would allow herself to be stroked and petted. They say she would even allow people to set a small child on her back and would hold still enough to have a photograph taken. Although I have not seen such a photograph, I believe the stories to be true.

She apparently did not take anyone for a ride. Since dolphins move so very fast, and since Old Speckledy Belly allowed only quite small children to sit on her back, I expect there would have been a terrified and half-drowned child, and a very frightened family, if she *had* taken off with a tot on her back.

By the early 1970's there was a camp with some facilities at Monkey Mia, with a permit from the shire, and a resident manager. Then late in 1975 the Mason family became interested in making a well-tended venture of the place. So they acquired it, and came to live there in late November of that year. Wilf Mason told me of his first visit to Monkey Mia.

"It was not much. Not very well cared for. But we could see the possibilities in it."

"Were you attracted to the place because of the dolphins?" I asked.

"No, we didn't know about the dolphins. No one mentioned them. The old chap who was here apparently didn't have any interest in them at all. When I came up here that first time to inspect the place, I did see them, but it didn't make much of an impression on me. I don't believe I even mentioned them to Hazel." He chuckled. "Little did I realize what an important part of our lives they would become."

Wilf and Hazel Mason came and began to make the place into a pleasant modern caravan park (we would call it a trailer park in America), with 75 sites, and an amenity block containing flush toilets, hot showers and a laundry, a generator for electricity that runs from seven in the morning until ten at night, and a small shop for a wide range of groceries and other necessities as well as a fair range of the luxuries that modern man has come to expect while on holiday. The park's spaces are full for only a few weeks a year, however, during Australia's May and August school vacations. Hazel and Wilf (a retired engineer) find it pleasant enough life.

The marvelous extra gift that they never realized they would find, however, is their friendship with the dolphins. In the years since they arrived, the friendship has mel-

lowed and deepened, and now the bond is very strong.
Every day except in the middle of summer, three to a
dozen dolphins appear close to the jetty, and will approach
anyone who comes into the shallow water at the beach. At
least six of them will take a fish from the hand and allow

themselves to be touched, and the Masons have given them names. Mother dolphins bring their small calves to the shallows, although, until they are at least a year old, they have not allowed them to be touched or fed fish. But they do suckle the little ones right there, and are perfectly at ease to have the small calves playing about all day near the camp beach.

When the Masons arrived at Monkey Mia, there was Old Speckledy Belly, who came to the beach regularly and took fish from the hand of anyone who offered it, allowing herself to be stroked on the beak or along the sides or back. Since she had almost no teeth, it is quite possible that it was not very easy for her to catch fish anymore. The closely spaced little conical teeth in a dolphin's mouth are not used to chew, but merely to grasp and hold the fish long enough for the dolphin to swallow. Without teeth to hold it, very likely the fish would be able to slither away, leaving a hungry dolphin. So perhaps Old Speckledy Belly was fairly dependent on the fish given her by the people at the beach; although from what I have heard and seen of dolphins, I imagine that other dolphins would have found a way to help supply the old lady with fish. An interesting fantasy.

At the time of Wilf and Hazel's arrival, in addition to Old Speckledy Belly, there were some other dolphins who came and went. There were a mother dolphin and tiny calf, they were charmed to notice. The mother, who came to accept a fish from the hand, was a particularly lovely pale grey dolphin, which they began to call "Beautiful." It was not long before they realized there was more than one calf among the dolphins that played about in the water not far from shore. They eventually realized there were two mothers, each with a suckling baby. The second mother came to be called "Holey-fin," and was easy to recognize because she had a small hole all the way through her dorsal fin. She also came in to feed and be touched.

Another very tame dolphin was named "Crooked-fin," because its large dorsal fin, when seen head on, was

distinctly curved over to the left at the tip. Other adult
dolphins would glide about in the water not far offshore.
Sometimes as many as eight dolphins altogether would be
present at one time.

Old Speckledy Belly stayed around as everyone's
friend for the first two years of the Mason's sojourn at
Monkey Mia. Then she ceased to come. As days and weeks
went by and she did not appear, they began to feel concerned, and as still more time went by, they realized she
would probably not return. A body was never found, but
now after three years of absence, they feel sure she is dead.
They have no reason to believe that her demise would not
be from natural causes as she seemed to be an aged dolphin.

The two young dolphins who were suckling babies
the first year the Masons were at Monkey Mia are now
adolescents, nearly five years old. They have been there at
the beach nearly every day of their lives, and now come
alone if their mothers do not happen to be coming on a
particular day. One of these is the most regular visitor of
all the dolphins, while the other sometimes is away for
several weeks at a time, and then comes again daily.
Crooked-fin's youngster, who is a year younger than these,
also comes independently of its mother now, and is a
faithful regular at the beach.

These three young dolphins, who have spent so much
of their time close to humans, give every evidence that
their contact with humans is as pleasurable to them as
their contacts with other dolphins. That is a very strong
statement, as contact among dolphins is clearly one of
life's greatest pleasures to a dolphin! In the pages of the
Journal I kept during my 1980 visit to Monkey Mia, which
forms the central part of this book, you will come to know
these three young dolphins quite well — their different
personalities as well as their individual appeal. You will
also come to know and love their three mothers, one of
whom has a new baby now.

But I am getting ahead of my story. Things had not progressed so far when I made my first visit to Monkey Mia in May of 1979. And even before I discuss that journey, let me cover a little background material.

2

What Is a Dolphin?

What is a dolphin? Most of us have impressions of a graceful, beguiling and jolly creature that lives in the ocean. Many of us, without really thinking, might say a dolphin is a fish, but if questioned further we might realize that we do know the dolphin is a mammal, giving live birth and suckling its young. Moreover, unlike a fish, a dolphin must breathe air, and although it lives in water, and cannot survive very long if not wet, it also cannot live more than about ten minutes at most without air.

The dolphin needs both air and water, so it lives in the sea, but comes to the surface every few minutes to take a breath. We all know how whales, which are close relatives of dolphins, come to the surface and spout to clear their air passages before taking a breath and submerging again. Dolphins also come to the surface and force air out through the blowhole in the top of the head (sometimes blowing a fine spray of surface water), then take a very fast gasp of air through the same hole before submerging again. We can get a feel for how this works when we use a snorkle, lying face down in the water and taking air in from above the head. Coming up from a dive, we blow to clear the tube and then take a breath. Dolphins do this with a very graceful movement that is beautiful to see. They come up from the deep, exposing the blowhole on the head, and the back with its curved triangular dorsal fin, then arch as they head down again to the depths, sometimes displaying the elegant tail with its flukes, which are parallel to the water's surface, rather than vertical like a fishtail.

Those of us who spend much time at sea are familiar with the sight of this graceful arching dark body in the ocean, and almost universally we take pleasure in the sight. We like to see a dolphin. We feel a lift to the heart. From the most ancient times sailors have considered it good luck to the voyage to see dolphins. It is as if the dolphin has given us a gift just being there.

Now we might ask, how is a dolphin different from a porpoise? Science classifies the "families" of whales, dolphins and porpoises into one "order" known as "cetaceans". In the United States the common names "dolphin" and "porpoise" have been used almost interchangeably to designate a number of different species of marine animals. In other parts of the world the word "dolphin" is used more consistently to mean small members of the cetacean order that have *teeth* (some whales do not have teeth) in a head that is *beaked*, while the word "porpoise" is usually used to designate one genus *(Phocoena)* of toothed small cetaceans that are *not beaked*. The dolphins I visited at Monkey Mia do have beaked faces, and are the same kind of dolphins we usually see in leaping and ball-tossing performances in the various sea circuses all over the world. The scientific name is *Tursiops truncatus* for northern hemisphere dolphins of this kind, and *Tursiops aduncus* for those in the southern hemisphere (there are slight differences in the number of teeth, etc.) It is only by this scientific designation that we can be really sure that we are all talking about the same creature. It is not actually incorrect to call it either dolphin or porpoise, then, as these are only common names, but most of the world knows this fellow as a "bottlenosed dolphin."

although the dolphin has no need to rely on man for any help, it seems always willing (and often mysteriously present at the right moment) to help man in distress in the sea. Exhausted swimmers have told of being bouyed up by a helpful dolphin. Many a mariner, throughout history and in modern times, has told a story of being guided out of harm's way by a dolphin.

One of the best-known records of a dolphin in more contemporary times is the case of Pelorus Jack, a New Zealand dolphin in the late 1800's that was accustomed to meet the ships that made their way among the intricate passages of the Marlborough Sounds at the northern tip of the South Island. Jack would appear between French Pass and Pelorus Sound, in sun or fog or storm, and go before the ship. He did this for many years and was regarded as a sort of mascot, until presumably the end of his life. When I make the trip on the "rail ferry" (called this because in traveling by train from one end of New Zealand to the other, you go on the boat for this watery stretch between North and South Island), I like to sit in the forward salon and watch for dolphins through the big plate glass windows, and think of Pelorus Jack. But I have not yet seen a dolphin there.

Beginning in ancient times, there have been many incidents of dolphins giving aid to sailors in difficulties at sea. Now in modern times such events occur frequently. In 1978 many newspapers carried the story of some men who were fishing from a small boat off the coast of South Africa. A fog formed, and as they tried to make their way through it, the fog grew more dense. They began to lose sense of direction and distance, and were unable to see the dangerous shoals which they knew were about them. As anxiety grew, they saw dolphins appear at their prow. The dolphins began to nudge the boat in one direction and another, guiding it through the treacherous waters! This continued for an hour and a half through the mists, with four dolphins guiding the boat until they reached safe waters. On shore at last, the men told news reporters of their dolphin escorts. One of the men, Kobus Stander, said, "We could not believe our eyes. How can you explain it? It was a great relief, and I will always be grateful to those dolphins."

When I was in New Zealand in May of 1980, just before going to Australia, a friend of mine was making a sailing trip alone in a small boat from Tauranga to near Whangarei, a trip of several days. On one particular day the way ahead seemed clear enough, so he set his course toward some low rocks in the distance and went into the little cabin to prepare some food. He told me, "Suddenly I had the thought that there were dolphins out there, and it seemed very important for me to see them. I dropped everything and went out, and there they were. It was quite wonderful to find them leaping across the bow from port to starboard. Then they went around and came back to leap across again in the same direction. It occurred to me then that they were telling me something! Perhaps they were warning me of the rocks ahead."

We mused over the fact that it was as if he had been *called* silently by the dolphins out of the cabin. Many people who work with dolphins in captivity feel that there is a strong element of silent communication with these animals. Or perhaps the high vibrational sounds they make are picked up by our ears at an unconscious level.

So we know that dolphins are sea mammals, which have, since ancient times, held a special place in man's thoughts and hearts. We know, too, that they have some special sensory abilities, discovered in more recent times. Realizing that the dolphin was able to be aware of objects, in detail and at considerable distance, even in murky water, humans investigated this phenomenon with captive dolphins in pools, and found that the animals send out sounds and learn from the echoes received, in the way that humans use "sonar".

It is easy for us to understand how this works, because we know something about sonar. But one wonders what would have happened if these investigations of the dolphins' gift of sound perception had taken place many years ago, before sonar was developed by man. Would we have been able to understand at all what the dolphin was doing? Yet dolphins have been able to perceive in this way for how many thousands of years?

The dolphin uses loud or soft and high or low frequency clicks as needed to discern details of close or distant objects. It can make sounds and receive them in extremely high frequencies, very far beyond the range the human ear can hear. It can send out up to 300 clicks per second and, of course, interpret the information during that time to learn about objects in the environment.

In one experiment, two steel balls were made exactly alike to the smallest tolerance except that one was hollow inside. The dolphin was able to choose which was which quite easily by using its echoing sound devices. (Heaven help the poor human who might try to deceive a dolphin with the old game of the pea under the walnut shell!) The dolphin can operate at an equivalent or better than some of the most sophisticated machines humans have devised. What we have done with our combination of brains and hands in building amazing machines outside ourselves, the dolphin has evolved naturally within its own body and nervous system.

Studies of the dolphin body and brain, and of its ability to communicate and understand, have provided scientists with an awesome collection of facts about the development of intelligence and adaptation to environment of this marvelous creature. They tell us that the stage of brain development reached 2,000,000 years ago by primates (ancestors of humans and modern apes) had been reached by dolphin ancestors some 30,000,000 years earlier.

Chapter seven contains more scientific information about dolphins, but at the time I visited Monkey Mia, I did not have that information. Therefore, in order to have the reader's understanding develop as mine did, we will go on now to tell some simple history.

3

My First Dolphin Experiences

Most of us have come to know something about dolphins because of a visit to a sea circus or "marineland" where dolphins are kept in captivity to put on marvelous shows for crowds of people. This is also the way I first came to be interested in dolphins thirty years ago.

We were living in Trenton, New Jersey during a very cold winter. I had grown up in Texas and, although I had spent several years in northern states, I still found the cold very difficult to enjoy, especially the fact that winter lasted so long. In my childhood the new spring leaves would come out on the trees in late February, and balmy days would be interspersed with few chilly ones from then on. On this particular year in New Jersey, the winter was especially cold, and one morning in mid-March, upon awakening to another day of fresh snow and freezing winds, my husband suggested that we take an unplanned vacation to Florida. I was pregnant, and we decided it would be our last chance for a vacation with no family responsibilities. His employer was agreeable, and the next day we set off. It was marvelous to get to the warm sun and sea, and to lounge on the open beach in the fragrance of tropical flowers.

At this time there was a new form of entertainment for Florida touists, a place called Marineland, where there were very large tanks containing sea creatures that could be viewed underwater through portholes as well as from the surface. There were enormous fish and turtles . . . and there were dolphins. Several times a day there was a "show," when a man at the edge of the tank called out various commands to a few dolphins, blew a whistle, fed fish from a bucket, and produced astounding results.

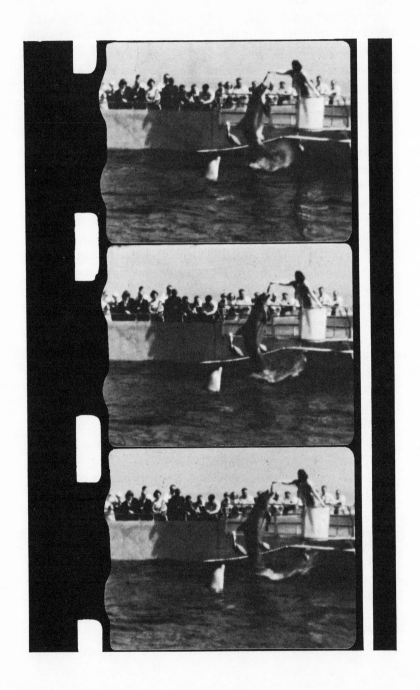

The dolphins leapt and dived, fetched and carried, swam in unison, and caught tossed fish, or came to the edge of the tank to take the reward gently from the trainer's hand. This was well before "Flipper" was on television, and since we had never heard of such a phenomenon before, we were properly thrilled.

Now, mind you, this was a scene very different from a present-day dolphin show. The tank was no more than perhaps 15 yards across, and the crowd simply stood around a fence at the edge of the pool. There was a tower at one point from which a hoop was dangled, if I recall, for the dolphin to jump through. Then the trainer climbed up the tower and offered a fish held by hand out over the water at perhaps ten feet above the surface, and the dolphin jumped up and took the fish. The crowd applauded enthusiastically. *Then* the man suggested that someone from the crowd might like to try offering a fish from the tower. Silence. My husband and I looked at each other. Oh, I wanted so much to do it. "Go ahead", he whispered, nudging me toward the man. No one else was volunteering, so I raised my hand tentatively. "May I?" I asked.

They wrapped me in a voluminous raincoat to prevent me from getting splashed, gave me a fish to hold by the tail, and up the steps I went. We had a little home movie camera, and I still have this sequence that my husband took. I held the fish out over the water as the dolphin circled and gathered speed. Then, just as it leaped up toward my hand, I grew a little frightened and jerked my hand up, so that the poor creature missed the fish, through no fault of its own. The trainer admonished me to hold still, assuring me that the dolphin would not hurt me. At the second leap the dolphin did indeed get its fish. Even after all these years I vividly remember the dolphin hurtling up towards me, and how I looked into its eye as it came even with me ... and the beautiful feeling of — well — making a connection with this lovely animal. I remember becoming suddenly very aware of the baby in my abdomen, and feeling that the dolphin sensed the baby's presence and acknowledged it. All this in a flash! So it was as if my little daughter, born some months later, was welcomed to this life by the dolphin.

There is another intriguing sequence on the film we took that day, which is of interest to my new friends who study cetaceans. There was one pool at the Marineland where a baby dolphin lived, and we very much enjoyed watching it at play, diving and rolling about in the water. I took a few moments of film of this dear little thing playing with a pelican feather which was floating on the surface. The baby dolphin would come up from under the water and catch the large feather in its mouth, tossing it up in the air, then dive under as the feather floated down to the surface. Then up would come the small dolphin to catch the feather and toss it again. It played at this game most charmingly for some time. Recently I have read that the first successful dolphin birth in captivity was at that Marineland at about that time, so it seems probable that the little dolphin we enjoyed watching was that very one.

My next experience with dolphins was some sixteen years later, when one of my nieces came to spend a summer with my daughter and me in California. Melody was a shy child of eleven years old who loved animals. We all went to visit Sea World in Mission Bay in San Diego, a new development at that time. There we saw a dolphin show that was a whole different order of magnitude from the one in Florida years before. The large lagoon held a number of dolphins, and the trainers employed many new tricks using fancy props to show the dolphins off. There was a big grandstand full of people, and all of us enjoyed the excitement very much. Melody was thrilled beyond words.

We also saw the show in another pool with Shamu, the so-called "killer whale," or orca. At this time Shamu was very young, nowhere near as large as she became later, and lived in a very limited basin of water. Her trainer was a young man who did a splendid job of explaining much about the beautiful orca, and how he worked with her to bring about the behavior that formed the show. Melody

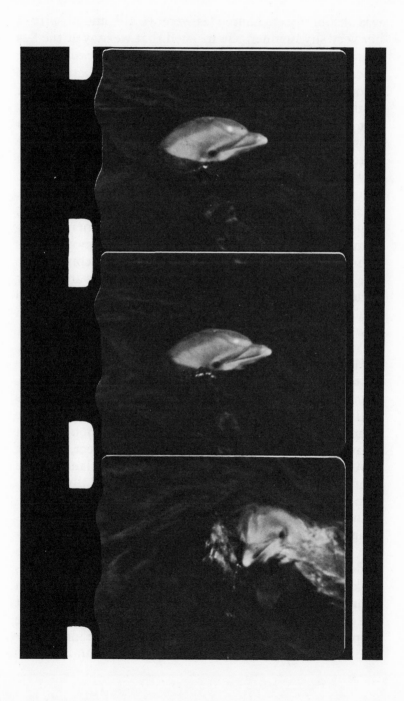

was absolutely enchanted (as were we all), and in spite of
her very shy manner, she insisted that we stay at the Sea
World park until the next time this show would take
place. So we saw the orca (a large dolphin, actually) go
through her routine again, the young trainer brushing her
teeth with a giant toothbrush, accepting a large and very
wet kiss on his cheek, and even putting his head in her
enormous and dangerous-looking open mouth. We
watched the orca circling the pool on her back, and even
saw a leap and splash which completely drenched the
youngsters who insisted on staying in the front seats of the
bleachers despite warnings by the trainer. After this show,
Melody urged me to take her to talk to the trainer, a young
man of Asian origin, who very kindly told us more details
of his friendship with this lovely animal, and conveyed to
us a deep sense of her intelligent, adventurous and loving
nature. I was as captivated as Melody, and after that always
read with much interest any articles that came out in
newspapers and magazines about dolphins and whales.

John Lilly's book, *Man and Dolphin*, published in
1961, came to my attention somewhat later, and I was
quite interested in his experiments with the dolphins,
Elvar and Tolva, and in the remarkable laboratory that was
built for them in the Virgin Islands. We had lived on the
island of St. Thomas for a year in 1951, and I thought what
a lovely place it was to work on such a project, wishing
that I had stayed a little longer on that small island to have
been there while the research was going on. Lilly's intention was to try to establish communication between humans and bottlenosed dolphins through sounds and language. The book described his studies of dolphin sounds —
the clicking, whistling and creaking sounds they make
under water, and the squeals and blats they sometimes
make in air. One of the difficulties in human-dolphin
communication with sounds, Lilly commented, is that
the airborne sounds we make cannot be heard well by the
dolphins under water, and conversely, we cannot hear
their underwater sounds above water, in the air. Lilly also

analyzed recorded dolphin sounds and detailed his interesting attempts to get the dolphins to "speak" English with what seemed to be some small success.

Later I heard that Lilly had set his dolphins free, and I felt a rush of pleasure. To me, that seemed the really significant point of the whole matter, and perhaps that was Lilly's feeling also. Could we somehow study dolphins without keeping them prisoner?

4

First Visit to Monkey Mia

Another interval of many years elapsed before I had any further contact with dolphins. Then in 1979 I was traveling around the North Island of New Zealand, camping here and there on the beautiful beaches and among the forests with my friend Kate. It was October, spring in the southern hemisphere, and the hills were brilliant green with little white lambs dancing in the sunlight. The small shrub known by the Maori name of manuka, which grows profusely over many of the slopes, was in bloom, its tiny delicate white blossoms giving the effect of a light dusting of powdered sugar, and lending the air a lovely fragrance. The coastline is indented again and again with small bays and inlets, sometimes with towering cliffs overhanging the sea, and sometimes with beautiful beaches stretching into the clear turquoise water. A little later, the great pohutukawa trees would be in red bloom, around Christmas time (early summer), but now they stood in solid masses of deep green on their gnarled old trunks beside the white beaches. We drove in our little Mini over hill and dale and came to the small beach resort town of Opononi.

"This is where the dolphin, Opo, lived," Kate told me. "Do you know about Opo?" I had not heard of this friendly animal who had taken to coming to the beach and playing with the children in 1955. We had lunch in a modest restaurant where there was some literature telling of the phenomenon. Opo was a young female bottlenosed dolphin who came into the shallow water where people would stand and pet her and play with her. One young girl especially was her favorite, and she would allow this girl to ride on her back. The dolphin came regularly to the beach from August of 1955 all through the summer (December, January, February). There was so much interest in the friendly dolphin that the town was overwhelmed with visitors. Hundreds of people would be on the beach, many standing in the edge of the water, trying to touch the lovely Opo. I saw one picture of a middle-aged man fully dressed in trousers and shirt with tie, up to his hips in the sea, stroking the dolphin.

She would toss a ball about for the children, and if no ball was available, she would bring up empty beer bottles from the sea floor, and toss them around! When people applauded her antics she responded by leaping out of the water joyfully. If anyone became too rough in handling her she slapped her tail on the water and moved just out of reach. She would not take fish offered by hand, but was able to catch plenty of fish for herself.

Then in March of 1956 Opo was found dead on the beach, and the general opinion is that she was killed by an explosion of dynamite, but it is not known exactly how. It was a very sad ending, and the townspeople of Opononi were joined by the people of all New Zealand in mourning their sea-dwelling friend.

Kate and I went out on the beach where there is a pretty sculpture of Opo. Standing there beside it and looking out over the water, it is easy to imagine a dolphin gliding in through the clear water to invite us to come and play. And how responsive the warm-hearted New Zealanders had been. There are only 3,000,000 people in all of New Zealand, but 1,000,000 of them live in Auckland, which is only a four-hour drive from Opononi, so it was

easy for them to come to visit Opo. I could imagine what a
magical experience it would be to have a dolphin swimming among us as we frolicked in the water, and I regretted
that I had not been there when it was happening.

It was only a few weeks later that I read an article
about dolphins in the beautiful magazine, *Simply Living*,
which is published in Australia. It was an account of a
place on the west coast of Australia where some dolphins
come in regularly to the beach, and people could feed them
and occasionally touch them. There were a few fine
photographs and an identification of the location, near the
town of Denham in Shark Bay, north of Perth.

I was planning to return to Australia, my third visit to
that enchanting country, and had thought that this time I
really wanted to get out to the west coast. Upon reading
this article, I resolved that when I did get to Perth, I would
surely take a little tour north to Shark Bay and see those
friendly dolphins.

At Easter time, then I took the train from Adelaide for
the very long journey across the plains of Australia to
Perth, where I was met by friends who asked what sights I
wished to see in western Australia. When they heard that I
wanted to go to Shark Bay to see some dolphins, they were
quite intrigued, but also amused to find that I had in mind
a little jaunt of a few hours or perhaps a day or two. What I
had not known is that it is 800 kilometers* (500 miles!)
north of Perth to Shark Bay, and there is very little transportation. They were both working and could not get away
to take me there. But the more I learned, the more I wanted
to go.

Whenever I describe to anyone the journey I made to
see the dolphins that first time, I get comments about the
great determination I must have had. It just seemed that
once I began to plan that trip, no matter what obstacles
arose, or how difficult it seemed, there was no way to turn
back.

I was on a very limited budget, and of course had no
vehicle of my own. When I learned that a bus would go

---

*The metric system is used throughout this book, because I became accustomed to it
in Australia, and Americans must learn it soon. There are approximately 8 kilometers
for each 5 miles. For a meter, think a yard.

only twice a week on the highway that passed some 130
kilometers from Denham, and that there is no public
transportation on to Denham (and to the fishing camp
called Monkey Mia, where the dolphins are, is another 24
kilometers beyond that), I began to inquire about the possibility of renting an automobile for the latter part of the
journey. I found that there were no car rentals up in that
part of the country at all, and I certainly could not afford to
rent one for the whole journey all the way from Perth. The
bus would arrive at an all-night roadhouse at the junction
with the road to Shark Bay at 1:30 in the morning, and it
appeared that the only way to get on out to the peninsula
was going to be to hitchhike. Well, maybe the roadhouse
had some motel rooms to rent, and I could sleep until
morning and try to catch a ride.

So I allowed eight days for the whole trip; and on the
23rd of April, 1979, I took the bus north from Perth, carrying my little tent and a few provisions and cooking gear.
The bus arrived at the roadhouse at an hour and a half past
midnight — and there was no room to rent. There was only
an all-night cafe, and some petrol pumps and rest rooms. A
more barren landscape I have seldom seen. Red earth, dry
as could be, with a few scrawny acacia-looking trees here
and there. I wondered vaguely about the possibility of
pitching my tent to sleep until dawn, but the earth looked
so hard, and not a blade of grass was to be found. I chatted
with the cook in the kitchen, and he told me that there
was a trucker who usually came with loads of various sorts
for the stations (farms) out on the peninsula, and for the
village of Denham. He would come on the night of the bus,
because there were sometimes packages to be delivered
from the bus, and usually he would come around this
time, sleep in his truck until morning, have breakfast and
go on his way about 6 AM. "He should be here any time
now, and you could ask him to take you out to Denham in
the morning. I'm certain he'll give you a lift." So I had a hot
chocolate and a sandwich and sat at the little table and
read.

It was a very long night of waiting, and the trucker never came. Finally after the sun was high, I decided I'd better not wait for him any more, but had best get out on the road to see if anyone else might be going that way. I had not seen one vehicle make that turn all night! Well, just as I was wearily gathering my things together, a truck drove up, and the driver came in and ordered breakfast. The cook spoke to him and nodded towards me. It was the regular man, behind schedule. He kindly did give me a ride, stopping at several places, once taking two hours to unload a delivery of lumber at a sheep station. The sun was very hot, and I felt very weary and longed for a shower and rest. Would I ever reach my dolphins?

Finally, arriving in Denham, I asked in the grocery store-post office, in the pub, and all around the tiny town if anyone knew of a possible ride out to Monkey Mia. The woman serving beer in the pub suggested that no doubt the Mason children would be picked up from school, and I sould inquire there. So I climbed the hill to the little schoolhouse, where children were playing in the yard at their noontime recess. Finding a woman watching them, I asked which were the Mason children. Two dark little boys were pointed out, and I asked them if they thought I might be able to ride home with them after school. With a shy smile they assured me it would be all right. What time would that be? 3:00. Another long hot wait. I thanked them, and turned away, and walked slowly down the hill looking over the blue bay in the white hot sun. At least I could wait by the sea.

But it seemed that the woman who had heard my wish to go to Monkey Mia was not a teacher but the schoolmaster's wife, and had the afternoon free. So in a little while, she appeared in her car with her small toddler, and offered to drive me. "It would be nice for the baby to see the dolphins out there." Angel of mercy. I gratefully got in, and we drove the 24 kilometers.

No doubt my weariness colored my experience, but my first sight of Monkey Mia was not inspiring. There is little vegetation — a few little trees with thin foliage widely spaced, bare red earth, and white seashell gravel to pave the driveways between the campsites. Hazel Mason received me very cordially in the small shop, and I told her I wanted a tent site for a week. They rarely have anyone arriving without a vehicle. I told her I had come to see the dolphins, and she was interested to hear that I had come such a long journey for that purpose, as nearly all their visitors come primarily for the fishing, although many also enjoy the dolphins. I was shown a campsite, dumped my things, and went down to the beach. No dolphins in sight. Hazel said they had probably gone for the day, "But you'll see them tomorrow." In spite of the hear, the water felt quite cold to my toes, and I wasn't feeling really hardy, so I didn't go in. I put up my tent and had a shower.

Wilf Mason came to find me. He is a sturdy man of medium height, sandy hair going white, and kindly blue eyes. He explained to me that only two weeks before there had been a "cyclone" (hurricane to Americans) that had done much damage to the camp. There were only a few jagged posts in the water where the "jetty" or pier, had been. Several of the camp sites had little tin-roofed shelters which were intended to provide extra area for anyone arriving with a "caravan" (trailer) or tent, and were now in various states of disarray. Near the site I had picked was one of these shelters which had been considerable damaged, but was still standing, and Wilf said I could use it without charge, if I wanted to clean it up a bit. I accepted gratefully. But cleaning would have to wait 'til tomorrow. At the moment all I really wanted to do, since there were no dolphins to see, was to have a little something to eat, and go to sleep. I made some food over a campfire, took a brief stroll down the beach in the sunset, crawled into my tent, and was fast asleep.

At dawn I was wide awake, as is my custom. In the grey light, through the netting of my tent's little window, I could see the fine foliage of the little tree I had crowded my tent against for some meagre shelter from the sun. I could smell the sea, mixed with that peculiar scent that is often found in deserts — a smell of dry earth, I suppose. I got up and went out to the beach eagerly. No dolphins — just the wide expanse of calm sea stretching away to the horizon, with a long curve of distant cliffs away to the left (northwest). All my weariness was gone, and I felt a very deep sense of delightful expectancy, and a surge of life energy. I skipped and danced along the beach to some distance from the camp, where I settled down and practiced my morning yoga under the wide sky, breathing the marvelous clean air, which felt especially laden with "prana" (yoga word for "life force" in the breath). How glorious to be here. How glorious to have a healthy body to stretch and slough off the cramps and strain of the journey. Cold as the water was (mid-autumn at this time), I plunged in and had a quick and exhilarating swim. Marvelous morning. "Now I am ready for you, dolphins."

But they did not come for some time. Quickly I cleaned out the sand and debris from the shelter and found it a good place to get out of the sun, and to keep my food from the flies without crowding my sleeping space. I was feeling very much at home. There were not many other campers — not more than a dozen campsites were occupied. One older woman who had a campfire burning outside a large family tent offered me a cup of tea in true Aussie fashion, which I accepted, and had a nice chat. Two small motor boats came in and pulled up on the sand, with men and boys and fishing gear.

But still there were no dolphins. I went in to the shop to buy a few groceries, and to get better acquainted with Hazel. She is a tiny, middle-aged, matter-of-fact, cheery woman with bright dark eyes that look directly into yours. Her own children grown and gone, she and Wilf had taken the two foster children I had seen at the school the day before. They are part-aborigines, and have been with them several years.

Hazel was interested to learn that I am a yoga teacher and said she would like me to give some lessons to the whole family. "Out here so far from any city, we don't get much opportunity for anything such as yoga lessons." I was very pleased to agree. She was also curious to explore the possibility of whether I might be able to communicate with the dolphins by meditation, and I said that I too had wondered about that, and that I intended to try.

And then the dolphins came. It was only a bit past 9:00, but it seemed as if I had been waiting forever. I walked out onto the beach where I saw a few children looking toward the water, and there were three dark grey bodies sliding through the clear green sea about three meters out, with triangular dorsal fins showing above the surface. They cruised slowly back and forth parallel to the beach, occasionally tilting to one side to lift an eye out of the water, and of course also occasionally raising a little higher to expose the top of the head with its blowhole in order to breathe. A lovely sight. There were two large ones and another about two-thirds their length, each swimming somewhat separate from the others. They showed obvious interest in us standing on the sand, and I marvelled that, with the open sea behind them, they had come here apparently just because we humans were here. One of the children, a boy about ten years old, seemed experienced in relating to them, for he waded in to knee depth and patted the surface of the water with his palm, saying, "Hello, Nick. Hello, Holey-fin."

The dolphins passed a few more times, eyeing him, edging closer; then one of the large ones angled in to glide right past him, barely an arm's length away. But reaching out, he could not quite touch it, and it glided on past. Another of the smaller children waded out into the water, and the dolphins continued to cruise back and forth, the smaller animal becoming a bit more animated — diving and surfacing, and speeding up in its passes. Then it made a big fast circle, and came right up to the boy, pausing in front of him just long enough for him to touch its beak, then with a swish, it glided away again. I made some excited exclamation, and the boy turned to me with smiling eyes, and said, *"You* can touch them!" I waded in and stood beside him, as did the other two children who were there. One had some small fish, which the children held by the tails, dangling just above the water. The first boy again patted the water repeatedly with his palm and called to the dolphins. Soon one of the large ones came again, and this time took a fish gently from a small hand, then glided away again. Then the other large one came and did the same. The children were dancing excitedly in the shallow water, and I was completely enraptured. It was really true, all I had heard about these dolphins.

The first boy had a fish now, and the smaller dolphin came for it, taking it from the boy's hand as he used the other hand to stroke the dolphin's beak. Then again the dolphin gave a great swish of its powerful tail to dart away very fast. But I noticed that it did not swallow the fish, but carried it around in its mouth as it swam in big circles. One of the fish given to the larger dolphins was floating in the water some distance away. Well, I thought, either they were not very hungry, or they dislike this kind of fish.

Soon the dolphins swam farther out, and lazed in the deeper water where it was more difficult to see exactly what they were doing, as they appeared only occasionally to breathe. It seemed to me that there was a fourth one, but I could not be sure unless they would all have surfaced at once. I went in to tell Hazel about it, and she smiled at my excitement. She said the smaller one must be Nick. "Does he have a nick right out of the top of his fin?" He did. I told her that they did not take all the fish the children offered, and seemed not to eat the ones they did accept. She gave me a bucket with three fish in it and said, "Here, offer them these. They especially like these bony herring."

So I went back to the beach, hoping they had not gone away. There were the two large ones, the younger one, and an even smaller one, which stayed fairly close to one of the large ones. Had it been there before, I wondered, without my noticing it? When I waded into the water, they approached closer, still coasting back and forth many times, parallel to the beach. One of the big ones came in close as I held out a fish, and lifted its beak out of the water with open mouth, gently closing on the fish and tugging it out of my grasp, then gliding away, and as the eye passed me, just under water, it looked into mine, and I felt — "Hello, old friend." It is a startling strange feeling of contact, at some deep inner level, that comes when you first really meet a dolphin.

I noticed that the back edge of this one's dorsal fin was quite ragged, and that there was a small hole right through the fin near its base. So this must be the one they call

Holey-fin, I thought, said to be the mother of three-year-old Nick. The other large one came close but did not take a fish. Holey-fin came back for another fish, and then came in again when I had no fish in my hand, and let me stroke her forehead, only briefly, and swam on past. The skin was a very unusual texture, rubbery and hard, but somehow with a give to it, and a warmth and vibrance that is difficult to describe.

Young Nick, who had been frolicking in the near shallows, then came for a fish, and took it rather more quickly from my hand, and raced away. I had no more fish, and set the bucket on the sand. When I waded back into the water, Nick came close past me again, and I reached out to touch his side, but he gave a great pump of his flukes and shot away from me, with his eye still on me though, so that I felt that he was amenable to more attempts

When they did not come very close again, but were still lingering only a few meters out, I decided it was time to try swimming with them. I put on my swim togs and headed into the water. It was quite cold, but the sun was so warm that I did not mind. I am a good strong swimmer, and headed straight out to where the dolphins were cruising in their customary lines parallel to the beach. I had this fantasy of swimming right in among them, and having them jostle me as I had seen them do to each other a few times. But that is not what happened. Dolphin eyes observed me, but there was not really a welcoming feeling to them. As I swam towards one, it would dive and disappear. Then as I turned to another, away it would go. Then the first would begin to swim in very fast circles around me a few times, perhaps two meters away, and when it took off another would swim towards me and then dive far under and come up on the other side. Sometimes they would come quite near on a speedy pass, but always stayed at least beyond my fingertips.

I love to swim, and ordinarily feel quite graceful and at home in the water, but I must say that in my attempts to swim with the dolphins I have never felt more awkward

and clumsy. And *slow*. As these lovely graceful creatures
glided and curved and dived and raced and danced around
me, I floundered and grasped for them and missed, and felt
like a clown among ballet dancers.

After a time, I felt just cold and dissatisfied, and came
out and got dressed. It was really more fun to admire them
from the beach. I watched them for a time, and then
realized that the large dolphin with the smaller one had
disappeared. This was about 12 noon. Within five minutes,
Holey-fin and Nick had disappeared as well. It seemed
strange to me that I could not see any dolphins surfacing
farther out as they swam toward the open sea. But this
happened day after day that they would leave in the same
way. They would be playing not far from shore, and then I
would notice that there were not as many as there had
been. But no dolphins were visible farther out. And when
one or two had gone, within a very few minutes all would
be gone for that day. It did not seem possible that they
could swim so far so fast or that, or that they would not
need to come up to breathe somewhere within sight. But it
did seem that when they decided to leave, they really took
off and *went*!

Next morning I was up at the first grey light of day,
and there were no dolphins. But by the time I had done my
yoga practice, the dolphins appeared with the rising sun.
They were doing their own yoga practice about five meters
offshore, bending, twisting, breathing. I only wished to
look half so graceful, and be able to do my stretches as
easily as they seemed to do. They stayed all morning, and
although I had no fish to offer, they came up to me as I
stood in the water knee deep. Another large dolphin, called
"Beautiful" by the Masons, allowed me to stroke and
pat her beak briefly. She was paler grey than the others, and
seemed especially sleek and elegant. Her name suited her
very well. They said she had a calf the same age as Nick,
but it was not with her. Holey-fin and Nick were there,
and another dolphin which did not come in close at all.

The other mother, who had been there the first day

with her calf, did not come, but I learned that she was called "Crooked-fin" because her dorsal fin curves over sideways at the tip. I went swimming again and had a similar experience of the dolphins swimming around me but out of reach, and not seeming to really welcome me.

Back on shore, I joined some people who were standing in the shallow water offering the dolphins some fish that had been frozen and thawed. The friendly animals would come in close enough to touch, but did not take the fish. Occasionally one dolphin, usually Holey-fin, would accept a pat, most often from a child.

After the other people had gone I tried whistling to the dolphins while they cruised back and forth. I am not very good at whistling, but they seemed somewhat curious about my sounds. I tried some long vocal sounds with deep resonance, especially the OM as used in yoga. I cannot say that they really paid much attention, but they did remain close, especially Nick, who glided back and forth along my part of the beach for some time.

Again they all went away around noon. It was very hot in the middle of the day, with no breeze, and I was grateful for the use of the shelter, to sit and read in the shade, screened from the infamous Australian flies. The Masons had given me their file of information about dolphins from magazine articles and correspondence with various people interested in dolphins. This was how I first heard of Wade and Jan Doak in New Zealand who founded Project Interlock, an organization to collect and disseminate information about dolphin contacts with humans. (I wrote to them at this time, and then visited them in New Zealand a year later, in April 1980.)

The days passed. I had no camera with me, but there were postcards for sale with a picture of the Masons' pretty 18-year-old daughter Sally (now living away on her own) shown feeding the dolphins, and I sent these postcards to all my friends. As the sun went low, I would stroll along the beach gathering shells, many beautiful gastropods, and a few pretty varieties of cockles and mussels. The

women and children of the camping families enjoyed finding shells while their men went out in boats to fish (although some of the women were as keen on fishing as the
men, and some of the children would fish too). I had a nice
conversation with one very small boy who had found a
particularly pretty bivalve with the two halves of the shell
still joined together. He had enjoyed playing with his
lovely toy for hours, inventing many games. But finally
the hinge had endured too much stress, and the two halves
had come apart. He had two shells now, but he mourned
the division and tried to press them back together. We
talked about how, when the animal was alive, the shells
had made a house for it, and only when it died did they
come apart. It is natural to be one, but separation also
comes to all of us.

After the child had gone to bed in his family's caravan,
I sat for a long time in the twilight on the beach, feeling the
gentle surge of the sea as the tide went out, and deepening
awareness of the multitudinous life in the sea. The fluid-
ity of a watery existence, with all its grace and lightness,
seemed very alluring. I imagined how it might feel to be
born a dolphin in that watery cosmos, surrounded by
loving family and friends. To spend a life gliding, diving
and catching fish, leaping, playing and rubbing against one
another. They do seem to have the most carefree and
joyous life of any creatures I could ever imagine. We humans seem to make life so complicated!

I would be at the beach at dawn every day, and at that
time the dolphins were never in sight, but usually came
around sunrise. During the week I was there, they were
always gone by noon, and never returned in the afternoon,
although the Masons said this was not always their pattern. They have seen them at night, but that is more
unusual. Usually only three to five came, but one day
there were seven. Holey-fin, Nick, Crooked-fin, her
young one, and Beautiful all had let me touch them by the
time I had been there three days, but never when I was
swimming. I also gave up trying to interest them in any

sounds except normal speaking as I would talk to a friend (I always had the feeling that they understood my conversation).

Often they would spend two or three hours in a very quiet mood, drifting and gliding back and forth not far from shore. Sometimes a dolphin would be out there when others were close to shore being petted or fed fish, and I could not be sure if it was a dolphin I knew, or perhaps some dolphin friend of theirs who never came close enough to get acquainted with us. Or perhaps there were several dolphins who came one at a time that way, but were not quite ready to be touched by humans.

On two occasions the mood was very vigorous and playful. The dolphins would come in to take a fish and then dash back out to deeper water and frolic with one another before coming in again for a brief touch. Once while this was going on, a small motor boat approached from out at sea, and Nick went out to meet it. He circled round it a few times as the people waved and called to him, then suddenly rose up on his tail in the wake of the boat and hovered there, dancing slightly from side to side with that delightful grin. Then he slid neatly back into the water and dashed round and round again. Of course we all gasped and exclaimed and applauded as he bobbed up and down with pleasure at our appreciation. What a ham! Another time I saw three of them — Crooked-fin, her baby, and Holey-fin — all leap out of the water together in perfect unison, the small one in the middle. It was so lovely and graceful to see. And there was something nostalgic about it to me: I remembered when I was a young girl and my mother and my aunt were showing me how to waltz.

I thought, how natural it is for these dolphins to do all these agile, graceful, coordinated movements. When we see them in a sea circus, we admire the trainers for their achievements, but really, I doubt any dolphin needs to be *taught* to stand on its tail or leap in unison with its fellows.

The Masons and I came together for yoga lessons morning and evening, and both Hazel and Wilf were apt pupils. The boys, Craig and David, were very supple, but had more difficulty staying attentive. It was very nice to have a little part in their family life.

Strangely, the boys showed little interest in the dolphins, while visiting children paid much more attention to them. And the family black dog, Pluto, usually ignored them. After all, they were always there. Once though, I saw him do something that the Masons say he does from time to time. One day he waded into the water as the dolphins were there and watched for a few minutes as the great grey bodies flowed back and forth. Then one of the dolphins raised an eye out of the water, slowly approached the dog, and paused as dog and dolphin gazed into each others' eyes for one special moment. Then both turned away, and that was all.

Early one morning I did try sitting on the sand for quite some time in meditation, letting go all busy thoughts, to see if the dolphins might have a "message" for me, but did not have any revelation. I thought there is probably not a message in words. At least not for me.

When my week came to a close, I was pleased not to have to go back the way I came. A young couple with a large vehicle, who had been camping there, were returning to their home south of Perth and offered me a ride which I gratefully accepted. As we drove along, they told me something which gave me a strange feeling. I had noticed that no one else ever went swimming, and I had thought that it was because the water was fairly cold. But they told me it was because there was a dangerous large fish lingering about the shore there. They could see this fellow deep in the clear water as they would approach the shore in their boat. They had thought that they should warn me.

"But you were having such a good time, and we didn't want to spoil it for you. It seemed the dolphins would protect you. They do say that dolphins will keep dangerous fish away from people."

This fish, I learned, is known as a "blowie," and has a mouth full of big sharp teeth, and is said to be fond of taking a chunk out of human flesh. Well, I was glad they had not told me, and was not very sure I wanted to know about it even then! Had the dolphins been protecting me? Was that why they used to dive under me sometimes, to drive away the blowie? Well, I would never know.

5

The Dolphins Lure Me Back

After my adventures with the dolphins, I told everyone about them everywhere I went, in Australia, in New Zealand and back in America. Most listeners were intrigued, and said they had never heard of any wild dolphins that come regularly in groups to the shore to be petted. I, myself, realized more and more that this phenomenon at Monkey Mia was truly unique.

In December 1979, not long before I was to leave California for New Zealand again, I saw on television the beautiful film, *Dolphin*. It showed several different situations where dolphins, both captive and free, were interacting with humans, including one sequence of a man who had built an underwater instrument similar to an accordion to play music to dolphins. There were wonderful scenes, taken underwater, of dolphins swimming around some scuba divers, the graceful creatures flowing and pausing and undulating and circling about the person deep in the water. The sound track was a marvelous documentation of the clicks and whistles made by the animals as they explored the human shapes and positions (and attitudes?) of their strange new companions in the sea. The divers described later, on board the boat, how it felt to have these sounds cascading over their bodies, as the dolphins took readings on them.

The film was made by Michael Wiese and Hardy Jones, and Michael was interviewed in the television studio afterwards. He commented that he was leaving a few days later to go to New Zealand to visit some people

there who are working with dolphins. I thought it might
be the Doaks, so I telephoned him and told him about the
Monkey Mia dolphins, thinking he might want to travel
on to western Australia, as long as he was in that part of
the world. He was interested in hearing of our dolphins
and wished he had known of them while making the film,
but regretted that he would not be able to take the time to
travel there. It turned out he *was* going to visit the Doaks
in New Zealand. Wade and Jan Doak are the couple who
had written to the Masons about their organization, Project Interlock, and I had read their correspondence while I
was at Monkey Mia. The Doaks have had some interesting
experiences with dolphins while sailing and scuba diving
in New Zealand waters. The purposes of their organization are: to help collect knowledge of human-dolphin
contacts, especially those initiated by dolphins; to learn
ways to make those contacts more satisfying; and to circu-
late this information in order to build more understanding, sympathy and concern for dolphins. I sent a message
by Michael Wiese that I too hoped to be able to see the
Doaks in a month or two. But events have their own way of
evolving, and it turned out to be longer than that.

When I reached New Zealand, I became involved as
usual with a round of teaching raja yoga retreats in various
places, and with camping and tramping around in whatever gorgeous scenery happened to be nearby. At Easter I
was to teach a three-day retreat at Nelson, and, since I had
been on a strenuous travel schedule about South Island, I
decided to take a few days alone on a beach at Takaka. It
was one of the most serene and lovely experiences of my
life, to be there where the pounding high tide came up
under the windows of my little cottage, and the low tide
left great wide stretches of sand to walk on, with an occasional huge boulder to explore around. It was very late in
the season and almost no one else was there, so I shared
my thoughts with shellfish and birds. Great mountains
rose up behind the low green hills, and one wet morning
they were crowned with fresh white snow, a rainbow

arched over them, and all was reflected on the wide wet beach. The name of this place, Pohara, is the Maori word for "beyond," and I felt I had truly gone Beyond.

Takaka is just at the base of Cape Farewell, at the northwest corner of South Island, and Farewell Spit stretches far out to sea across the horizon. One day I took the tourist bus for the long, long ride out to the lighthouse at the tip. On the way we came upon two dead pilot whales lying up on the sand. The driver stopped for us to get out to see them, and I stood a long time beside one, with my hand on the great black body, wondering why it happens that cetaceans sometimes beach themselves this way. Could they be seeking something here on land? I have heard speculation that they may have some deep species-memory of a watery passage that once was here, and that would fit in this instance, for the long sand spit is fairly new in geologic time.

Back in North Island in early April, I made a visit to the Hawke Bay area, which I had never seen before. On a sunny afternoon the train brought me to the seaside city of Napier, and I found a nice little bed and breakfast accommodation across the street from the Marineland. Through gaps in the fence I could see dolphins leaping in their pool as a loudspeaker announced the start of the show. I was determined that I would see the 10:00 show in the morning.

But the next day was pouring rain. I had to travel that afternoon, so it seemed that the only chance for me to see the show was in the rain. The attendants handed out umbrellas to our hardy group of tourists undeterred by the weather, and we stood on the bleachers, not enough of us that the umbrellas would block anyone's view. This Marineland had the smaller "common dolphins," which abound in these waters, and as they enthusiastically leaped and danced and fetched and carried, the announcer told us that the animals here had all been rescued from strandings or injury, and that none of them had been taken captive as healthy animals from the sea. The trainers were very young men and women and seemed to have close bonds to the performing dolphins and seals. One baby fur seal was especially adorable, responding to the young trainer's coaxing by rolling over and then galloping back to get its fish reward. The small group of drenched viewers loved the show, and the animals obviously enjoyed the appreciation hugely. Since they were wet anyway, they probably didn't even notice the rain, but I wondered if a dolphin ever got raindrops in its blowhole, and concluded that the blowing function must succeed in clearing any water that might ever enter the respiratory system.

When I finally made a determined effort to see the Doaks in mid-April, an interesting and somewhat mysterious experience occurred. I was trying to get to Ngunguru, the tiny village on the coast north of Whangarei where the Doaks live. Just as a meeting was ending at a yoga retreat center near Auckland, one of the participants overheard me asking on the telephone about buses to Whangarei. "I am driving to Whangarei," he said, and offered me a lift, which I gratefully accepted.

The man's name was Herman Otto. In conversation on the long drive north, he asked me my purpose in traveling to Whangarei. I explained that actually I was going on north of Whangarei, and would be looking up some people interested in dolphins, Wade and Jan Doak. He glanced at me sideways in amazement. "At Ngunguru?" he asked. "I live at Ngunguru. The Doaks are my neighbors and best friends!"

So he drove me directly there, and as we walked up the hill to their house, a man working in the garden straightened up and recognized his friend Herman, and came to greet him.

"This is Chi-uh Gawain," said Herman in introduction. Now it was Wade's turn to be astonished. "Chi-uh? Who wrote to us from Monkey Mia? Where did *you* find her?" So we had to tell him about the strange coincidence of our meeting. "How wonderful to have you come. We are so eager to hear first hand about the dolphins there."

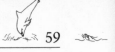

We all spent a long lovely afternoon over tea, exchanging stories of our dolphin friends, and next day went for a sail in their catamaran, with yet more conversation, but sighted no dolphins. They told me of the time when they were diving and had been approached by dolphins who swam with them and created a most beautiful feeling of kinship. Then a whole year later they happened to be sailing in the same area, and were again approached by the same dolphins! They recognized them by fin and fluke marks that they had noted the first time. Again they spent a wonderful day of communing and playing with the dolphins. Their records show that it was on the very same calendar day exactly a year before that they had first seen them! You can read about this, and other fascinating dolphin stories, both their own and others' in their new book, to be published soon.

All this talk served to whet my appetite even more to return to Monkey Mia. I was planning my next trip to Australia, and felt more and more drawn to go out to see my old dolphin friends again.

Meanwhile, however, the Great Barrier Reef had first priority. I had been there very briefly the year before, and felt I must have a more lengthy stay. One of the great joys of a life of "retirement" is that I am not confined to two-week vacations. So I managed to spend two months in Queensland, enjoying the gorgeous underwater magic at every opportunity, as well as the splendid rainforests. I revelled in the balmy air and relished the luscious tropical fruits.

At this time I was reading *The Lure of the Dolphin* by the English author Robin Brown. There is a lyrical description of how human and dolphin ancestors had been among those mammals that survived the cataclysmic demise of so many of the earth's creatures in the Cretaceous period, when the dinosaurs vanished. Nature's new invention, mammals, proved relatively efficient in survival, and went on to develop into the many mammals we know (and are!) today. One interesting fact in contrasting the evolu-

tion of dolphin and man is that 25,000,000 years ago there
was already a recognizable cetacean in the sea, while the
ancestor of man was still a bug-eyed, bushy-tailed tree
animal, not at all recognizable to a layman as the forerun-
ner of the human.

This book is packed with fascinating very recent information, as well as some intriguing musings about the
relationship of dolphins to humans.

Brown was concerned about the U.S. Navy training
program for dolphins. One of their dolphins, Tuffy, became
quite famous. He was very reponsive to training. The
Navy used him as an underwater messenger to the men in
Sealab (astronaut Scott Carpenter was one of the participants) in an experiment where humans lived at very great
depths in the ocean. The dolphin was able to make dives to
the depth of 200 feet and back as easily as the daring young
man on the flying trapeze, and also to locate and carry
objects in deep murky water. Later two orcas were trained
and, being bigger and stronger, performed marvelous
fetch-and-carry chores for the Navy with some heavy
equipment in deep water. But one day, one of the orcas
swam away. And some time later, the other stopped doing
as requested, and his training was ended.

Brown was concerned that the Navy might have been
teaching the dolphins to attack and destroy humans, and
he urged his readers to join in raising urgent objections to
any such training. I join my voice in strongly objecting if
such a program is going on, or even contemplated. I feel
that would be truly wrong.

The Navy has consistently and publicly denied that
they are doing or ever have done this. I realize that it would
probably be possible for them nevertheless to carry on
such a program secretly. In secret from the human public,
that is. But the dolphins would know, and I do not believe
they could be made to kill humans. Even if they were
tricked, I believe they would know the intentions, and
would refuse. Perhaps that was why the orcas went AWOL,
though Brown suggested that such repetitive tasks were

too boring for their intelligence. Perhaps there was something more ominous in store for them, and they knew it.

Of course, with no more information than I have, I cannot know with certainty, but I feel much confidence that dolphins would know if they were to be taught to kill humans, and would refuse to perform. Let us hope so.

Another passage in this book that intrigued me was the discussion of the "neoteny" factor. Brown says it is used by zoologists in judging the intelligence of different kinds of animals, and describes it as a quality of playfulness in mature stages of life. It takes intelligence to be playful after one is no longer a child! Well, the dolphins certainly are playful at all stages of life. I pondered these things as I walked the sands at dawn each morning at Port Douglas, at the Great Barrier Reef.

Occasionally, I like to try my hand at painting watercolor scenes, and one day while sitting on some rocks at the edge of a fine beach near Port Douglas, I was about to paint the blue bay into my little scene, and thought, "Wouldn't it be nice to have a dolphin in the water for my picture." I made a few more strokes on the sky, and looked up to compare the effect, and — there they were! two dark bodies arching through the clear water 100 meters out. It was so good of them to appear in the scene. They make the perfect accent for my painting. The only time I ever saw dolphins in northern Queensland was that moment when I called them in my mind to appear in the scene I was painting.

Another time I saw dolphins on the east coast of Australia, but much farther south. My California friend, Alma, had come to meet me for a few weeks, and we took the ferry to Great Keppel Island. We were carrying our backpacks and gear along the beach to set up tents in the campground, when we noticed a dolphin coming up for breath in a wave not five meters out. It coasted along parallel to our walk for a little time, and then another appeared just to one side and slightly behind it, as they so often position themselves. They both seemed to look at us as they slid easily through the water for a few minutes, then plunged under and reappeared farther and farther out, and were gone. Alma and I stood spellbound, then glanced at each other in delight at our welcome to the island, knowing that with such a beginning we would have a fine stay — which indeed we did.

We learned from some of the local people that dolphins had been seen quite often this year, and frequently accompanied the ferry as it took the holiday crowds around the island to see the scenery before depositing them on shore. I could well imagine that the dolphins would be attracted by the ferry's custom of letting out a "boom net" for the passengers to have a splash. This is a large and sturdy net which hangs from a pole extended out from the side of the cruising ferryboat. Hardy souls enjoy putting on their swim togs and clinging to the net as it splashes through the water. It is just the sort of thing that

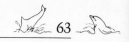

dolphins would enjoy taking part in, and I confidently predict that, unless something happens to put them off, the dolphins will be cavorting along-side the boom net full of tourists within a year or two. What a lark for all. A gift of fun to be exchanged between the dolphins and the humans.

During these several months, the Masons and I had been corresponding, and when I received a letter explicitly inviting me to return to Monkey Mia, I made a definite decision to go. In August of 1980 I returned to Perth, this time allowing two weeks to spend at Monkey Mia with the dolphins. The word from the Masons was, "try to come any time except between the 22nd of August and the 5th of September," because those were the weeks of school spring vacation when the caravan park would be full, and they would have little time to spend with me. But it happened that my schedule of teaching yoga was such that those very two veeks were the only time I was able to go to western Australia! Well, it would have to do. They said to come anyway if it was inevitable, and they would make a space for me. One advantage was that I would have the opportunity of seeing the impact on the dolphins of the largest holiday crowds of people appearing there annually.

I was not looking forward to a repeat of last year's long bus trip and night vigil waiting for a ride out the peninsula, so I was overjoyed when a telephone call came where I was staying in Perth, and Wilf Mason's voice was on the line. "I am in Perth for supplies, and can give you a lift to Monkey Mia."

It was good fortune not only to be more expeditiously conveyed to my destination, but also to spend the many hours of driving time talking with Wilf, because, as it turned out, both the Masons were desperately busy during those next two weeks, taking care of all the holidaymakers in the caravan park. Wilf and I made the most of our talking time, as we drove along.

It was at this point that I began writing the journal of my 1980 visit to Monkey Mia.

6

Journal 1980

Thursday 21 August 80

   Wilf and I made the most of our time talking as we drove from Perth in his heavily laden truck, with a trailer behind carrying more supplies for the busy holiday fortnight ahead. It was a beautiful early spring day (similar to a day of late February in the northern hemisphere, in a mild climate such as California.) Wilf told me that all our old dolphin friends are back this year, except that Beautiful's calf, now nearing five years old, does not come very often. It is nearly full grown and independent of its mother. However, Nick, the same age, comes every day. He told me, "There is one new dolphin that has begun coming to take a fish occasionally. I call it 'Snubnose'." It was very good news to hear that our group of touching dolphins is increasing. I was also excited to hear the details of Nick's baby sister (or brother?), Holey-fin's new calf, brought in the end of December. Wilf said that a week ago they had seen the largest number of dolphins ever at one time at Monkey Mia. They had counted 15, all romping and playing together in the water, and some coming to the beach as usual. Last year the most they had ever seen at one time was 11. Wilf said that each year, when the dolphins have their season of coming infrequently, he and Hazel wonder if they will come back. Some day they may not. But thus far, every year there are a few more dolphins, and we hope that will continue to be the pattern.

I asked some details about the time of absence. He said that beginning in mid or late November, as the very hot weather approaches, they cease to come daily; but the "regulars" usually come once or twice a week. Sometimes they see no dolphins at all for as much as three weeks. Sometimes when they go boating, they see them farther out in the bay even when none are coming to shore. This continues through December and well into January. Then by February they come more and more frequently as the season cools, until their daily pattern is re-established. Since there is no time when they are away for more then three weeks, it seems they cannot be going very far, and certainly not migrating. Perhaps it is a time of mating and/or birthing. It *is* a time when new babies appear, and since gestation is said to be about 10 to 12 months, mating must also occur during this time. "It is a time of hot weather as well," Wilf commented, "and very windy. Possibly the hot dry wind has something to do with it. And the water is lower at that time in our part of the bay. It could be that food is not plentiful, because the yellowtails are spawning, and they have a sort of slime on them. The dolphins will not eat them then. Even if we freeze them and offer them to the dolphins later, they will not eat them." So there are many factors that may contribute to the dolphins' absence during this season.

I told Wilf about my visit with the Doaks, and he said the Doaks had already written them and had included a draft of my stories about the Monkey Mia dolphins. They wanted to include them in their book and asked the Masons for their comments. One of the stories was about the "dangerous fish" called a blowie that had been in the water where I was swimming last year and how the dolphins may have protected me. Wilf was inclined to feel that I had not been in much danger. He called this fish a blowfish, blowie, or toadfish. It has a mouth rather like a parrot and *can* bite hard enough to take a chunk of flesh, but is "not likely" to do so. "I know a man who lost the tip of his finger taking a hook out of the mouth of a blow-fish he caught. It has sharp teeth and a strong jaw, but that doesn't mean the fish would attack a huge object such as a human." I felt inclined to agree.

"Our bay has a number of potentially dangerous species, such as sea snakes and sharks. But there is no need for anyone to assume they will do us harm. Snakes will come up close to *see* you, but not bite. My son's diving teacher showed him how he could touch the snake's head and turn it to one side, then to the other. He told him, if a snake is coming towards you, stay still. If you splash around, the snake will come to *see*. It might bite to protect a nest, but probably not otherwise." It is interesting how man is so often afraid unnecessarily.

It was lovely driving along on this sunny day of early spring in Western Australia. It had been a year of much more than usual rain, and the spring wildflowers, always renowned in this area, were outdoing themselves. The rolling hills were lush bright green, a contrast to the drab brown of the landscape when I had been here before in the autumn. Patches of pink or yellow now dotted the fields of green, and delicate flowers clung to the scrubby trees. "Just wait until we get farther north," Wilf said. The earth is covered solid with flowers, mostly white ones. It has been so wet that I think seeds that have been dormant for years must have sprouted. We even have weeds around the campsites at Monkey Mia," and he arched his eyebrows for emphasis. I could scarcely imagine that barren red earth with any greenery.

Actually, by the time we reached the area where there were thick carpets of flowers beside the road, night had already fallen, but the masses of white showed clearly even in the darkness. Wilf stopped the truck so that I could get out and stand among them. It was magical to stand in the dark warm night breathing the delicate fragrance of the white flowers spreading out before me, up and down over hill and vale. The stars spread across the sky seemed a reflection of the flowered earth. Nature's moods and seasons have so much variety of pleasure to offer us if we are ready to notice them.

Riding on, Wilf told me of a couple who had been staying at the caravan park recently. The man is a champion "footie" player (the game Americans call "soccer" is called "football" in Australia, and the Aussie penchant for diminutives converts it to "footie"). He and his new bride were taking a year off to travel around Australia. They had heard of the dolphins and came to Monkey Mia for that reason, intending to stay for a few days, but when they fell in love with the dolphins, they stayed a whole month. "He and Nick were great friends" Wilf told me. "The man would hold his hands in a big circle, and Nick would swim through as the man clutched and tickled. Then Nick would turn and swim through again. The woman wept when they left. I am certain we'll see them again one day, even though they live in far-off Melbourne."

He told me that many campers who stay perhaps a fortnight come to speak of "my dolphins." "They'll write months later to make a booking to come to stay for another holiday, and at the end of the letter they'll ask, 'Are my dolphins still coming in every day?' " I laughed at his tone. "Whose dolphins are they, Wilf?" He chuckled. "Well, I

always think they are *my* dolphins," he said, pressing his hand against his chest. I guess they belong to all of us."They have given themselves as a gift to us all," I said. "We feel it as a personal treasure just to be in their presence." We rode on through the night, silently musing on the marvelous feeling so many of us experience in the dolphins' company.

"Nick is becoming the star of the family," Wilf told me. "He is a great show-off. It is very obvious that he does more leaping and playing and standing on his tail when there are more people to watch him. He is there all day every day when we have many people in the camp. This week of holiday crowds will probably be a great treat for him. He's greedy, too. He pushes at the others to try to get all the fish that are offered.

"The other day he bit me."

"Really?" I asked in surprise. "Hard?"

"No, just a nip, but it broke the skin. I was feeding him a few fish from a bucket, and when the fish were gone, he was still crowding me for more. I said, 'That's all, Nick. No more,' and he grabbed my hand in his mouth. He does that sometimes, just as a friendly way to hold me, but this time he pulled and tore the skin a bit."

We talked a little about his and Hazel's concern that human contact could have any ill effects on the dolphins, especially the young ones who have now spent their whole lives in almost daily contact with humans. The Masons have succeeded in getting the government to appoint Wilf a "warden," an honorary position, with no salary, but it gives him the power to enforce the protective laws. The stretch of beach just west of the boat launch (the area where the dolphins most often come) has been posted to keep boats away, and a government signboard declares that all dolphins, seals and dugongs are protected here, noting fines for

molesting them in any way. These are important
steps.

The Masons would like to do more. Wilf asked
me if I knew of any possibility of getting a grant
from some organization interested in wildlife. I did
not know, but wanted to hear what he would like to
do if he could get it. He told me they were now
drawing up papers to create a foundation for
protection of the dolphins, and then they want to
have two things. First, an employed warden, who
would stay on the beach when people are feeding
and petting the dolphins, to give information and
see that no harm is done. Wilf would like to do this
himself, but must make a living, and the time when
the largest number of people are there (most
needing the warden) is the very time he must be
elsewhere on the property attending to camp
business.

Second, an educational exhibit. This would
require some sort of small structure with a room to
display pictures and explanations about dolphins in
general and these dolphins in particular, possibly
with some history of how this friendship has
developed. Perhaps there could be a continuous
slide show. But it could be quite simple. People need
to be told what is proper to offer a dolphin to eat (not
bread, for instance), and what else to do with a
dolphin besides feed it. There could be an
explanation of the sounds they make, and of their
perceptive gifts. Eventually it may be possible to
have a small library for those with a deeper interest.

It all sounded very good to me, and I was
pleased to hear that much progress had been made.
Wilf brought up the question of what would happen
to the foundation if "our" dolphins were to stop
coming one day. This is always a possibility.
Perhaps the charter can be worded in such a way
that whatever is generated by the foundation can be

used in that case for aiding harmonious human-dolphin contact elsewhere in Australia.

I told him about Robin Brown's book, *The Lure of the Dolphin,* and we talked about some of the phenomena described there. There was a photograph of two dolphins leaping through a suspended hoop from opposite directions, and passing one another exactly at the center. We mused over how skilled their coordination must be, and how exact the communication must be between the two animals. We imagined two humans attempting to learn the stunt of simultaneously jumping through a hoop from opposite sides. It would probably take many, many hours of practice, as with trapeze artists. More comparable would be a stunt where two persons would dive into the water and meet exactly to pass one another from opposite directions through a loop, changing from air, our natural medium, to water. But it is not really comparable, because it is much easier to control speed and direction in the water, in order to meet perfectly, than while hurtling through the air as these dolphins were doing. And they say the dolphins learned it very quickly.

We stopped at the all night roadhouse where I had spent such weary hours last year. It was pleasant this time to have a hot drink and a sandwich and be able to drive on. Wilf was trying to reach Monkey Mia before the generator went off at 11:00. We came over the hill and looked down on the twinkle of little lights among the tents and caravans, like a small town. Hazel gave us a warm greeting, and hurried me off to my empty caravan while there was still light to find my way.

Good to settle into my bunk. And tomorrow I can see "my" dolphins again!

Friday 22 August 80

Grey dawn. High tide. Still air. No dolphins in sight. After boat activity starts, the dolphins come in, and by 7:00 there are seven of them to greet me my first day! Last year that was the most I ever saw.

I feel quite excited to be back at Monkey Mia and to see the dolphins. It is so amazing to have these great creatures glide gently right up to within inches of my feet within seconds of the time I wade into the water! I stand at a depth only halfway up my calves, which is extremely shallow for a bottlenosed dolphin. It can scarcely maneuver its large body. As two come up to me and lift their beaks out of the water, mouths open, I look to identify who they are, from memories of last year. Oh, this is Nick, easily recognizable by the large nick right in the tip of his big dorsal fin. He is much larger than he was last year, almost as large as his mother, Holey-fin, who is also here. She too is very easy to recognize, as she has a very small round hole right through her fin, as well as a big scallop out of the back edge of the fin.

There are six children ranging from four to eight years or so, and a couple of other adults besides myself. The fishermen's nets this morning have already provided a few fish which are being given to the dolphins by the little group of people in the shallow water. I have no fish to give, so I reach out to stroke the grey beak passing near me, but Nick quickly swishes away. Who is this other one? Is it Beautiful? There is a pretty pattern of symmetrical, dark, grey longitudinal streaks along the pale grey head. But no, the big fin is distinctly bent to one side at the tip. It is Crooked-fin. And who is this other adolescent, about the same size as Nick? No marks on the fin, but a white scar near the blowhole with a tail on it like a comet. (Later Wilf says it must be Crooked-fin's "baby" who is

three and a half. The mark is probably from an ulcer.)

By this time I have noticed Holey-fin's new baby! At eight months old, it is already about three-quarters of a meter long, with a smooth, clear grey body slipping through the water, the epitome of grace. The others prevent it from approaching in

where we could touch, so it plays nearby, often
leaping out of the water in a half roll and exposing
its lighter grey belly. The others nudge and tumble
it often, and all roll around in the water together.
Hazel and Wilf have appropriately named the baby
"Joy".

Two other dolphins hang around at about four
meters out — one with a very ragged back edge to
the fin (shall we call it "Rags?"), and one with a deep
notch just behind the tip of the fin ("Notch?"). they
cruise back and forth parallel to the beach,
watching. I had not seen these two last year.

So nice to be with the dolphins again! The
fishermen offer me some of the bait catch from the
net, and I hand out about five fish. At first the
dolphins will not let me touch them, but after I
have tried a few times, I get in some strokes as they
pass, along the beak and down the side. The
children and one man are also petting them. They
tend to duck away and give their tails a mighty
swish to get out of reach when anyone tries to touch
the *back*, even if well behind the blowhole.

Many fish are fed, until finally the dolphins
begin to play at the feeding game, only mouthing
the fish and toying with them, then dropping them
in the water. Gulls gather, enjoying the discarded
fish. Still the dolphins would come to take any fish
offered by a hand. A father holds a child in his arms
who feeds a fish to Crooked-fin's offspring, while
the child's mother takes a photograph. This is such
fun that the father decides to try it with his smaller
child, surely not yet two years old, and the baby and
father both crow with delight. This time I too have
my camera ready, and believe I have a lovely
picture.

Fish thrown toward the two dolphins farther
out are not taken. Those two seem only to watch,
and join the party in spirit.

When no more fish are offered, all the dolphins drift farther out, and cruise back and forth. I feel concern that their principal contact with humans is feeding. Can't we find some other communication? Might Nick, for example, who has been fed to satiation every day of his life, get too dependent on feeding? Wilf has also expressed this concern. Is Nick really good at fishing for himself? We cannot know for sure. I'd like to try giving them a ball to play with. Wilf thinks it might be all right if we do not try to *train* them to do anything. Hazel is against it. I'd like them to be interested in other things about humans.

By 10:00 only Holey-fin and baby are there. By 10:30 all are gone, out of sight.

After 5:00 in the afternoon we can see dolphins playing languidly 200 meters out, drifting and arching slowly, and occasionally leaping. By 5:30 several come in close to shore. A brown shaggy dog of medium size stands in the shallow water quietly

watching them, and they swim right past him at
close range. A boy comes with a bucket of fish and
feeds the dolphins. A man stands in the water and
tosses a red tennis ball up and down in his hands.
Nick eyes the ball while gliding back and forth,
with one eye out of the water, then the other. But
when the ball is dropped in the water and left for ten
minutes, they pay no attention to it. Captive
dolphins enjoy playing with balls very much and I
wonder why these dolphins don't give it a try.

At 6:00 there are nine dolphins within five
meters of shore, but only four taking fish from the
hand, in the sunset:Holey-fin, Nick, Crooked-fin
and her offspring. By 6:15, all are gone, out of sight
in the far reaches of the sea.

Over tea, Hazel and I resume our friendship of
last year, sitting in their large pleasant room which
serves as lounge, dining room and kitchen, with a
door into the little shop which is the only store for
visitors and tenants in the caravan park. It is such a
pleasure to be with tiny bright eyed Hazel again!

She and Wilf tell of the arrival of the new baby
the last week in December 1979. As usual during
the hot season of the year, the dolphins had been
absent off and on. Then one day Holey-fin appeared,
with the new baby. There was great excitement in
the camp when the tiny one was noticed. It could
not be more than two weeks old, as they'd seen
Holey two weeks before. Hazel and Wilf waded out
to see, and she came right to them, just as she
always has done, but now she brought the brand
new baby close beside her! They stroked Holey-fin
exclaiming their pleasure and admiration, and she
allowed the baby to swim right between the two
humans as they stood in the water. Imagine the
mother, so soon after giving birth, bringing her
dearest treasure to share with the strange land
creatures. Even in telling me, Hazel is moved

almost to tears at the honor, and marvels at the
trust shown. "You know they say they are usually
very protective of their babies even when born in
captivity." It truly is a beautiful testament to the
human-dolphin friendship that has blossomed
here.

The other event they are excited about
occurred only two-and-a-half weeks ago, when they
counted 15 dolphins, the largest number ever
recorded at Monkey Mia. They and several other
people went out to swim, and the dolphins milled
around them, playing (though as always here, not
allowing themselves to be touched by any person
swimming). They stayed for quite a long while, at
least two hours.

"Watching from the jetty," Hazel said, "we saw
the dolphins rolling over one another. We felt sure
one was Beautiful's Baby" (B.B., now four-and-a-half
years old, whom they had not seen for several
months). "Beautiful was there, and as other
dolphins rolled over and over her, I wondered if they
were mating." Or was it just a party, that they
allowed humans to witness?

I told them about the man tossing the red
tennis ball at the water's edge this afternoon, and
how the dolphins made no attempt to play with it.
Hazel feels strongly that it is best not to teach them
to play with objects we offer them." Any action of this
type will change them from the way they exist at the
present moment. The dolphins are coming to meet
the humans, and it is a fine experience on both sides.
Once we start in any way to train them to play *our*
games, we alter the situation. I feel it would be better
to maintain things as they are for as long as possible."
long as possible."

Both Hazel and Wilf are deeply curious to
know: "What is the message? Why do the dolphins
come here? They come for fish, but it seems they

really come to be with us. Can you find out through meditation with them?" I'll try, and see.

Sat 23 August 80

At 6:15 of a windy dawn, there are no dolphins present. By 6:40 there is the first boat movement. Still no dolphins come. Full light and little choppy wavelets, but no surf (there is almost never any surf here this far into the bay). It's chilly! Brrr.

6:50 . . . sun-up. Six dolphins! Brown-dog is standing in the water. I wade in, and the faithful five dolphins come to see me: Crooked-fin, Puck (as I had decided to call Crooked-fin's adolescent), Nick, and Holey-fin with her baby, Joy — but Joy is always crowded away from being touched by humans. I give them each a quick rub under the chin and say, "Hello, Crooked-fin . . . good morning, Nick."

On this second day of my visit they do not hesitate to let me touch them, even though I have no fish for them, and I feel a flood of loving closeness to them.

They drift back out to play. Joy leaps out of the water and twists to belly-up before re-entering.

Who is that sixth dolphin? I cannot make it out.
They're off to the left near the boats, and Brown-dog
wades out toward them. They ignore him, but
tolerate him. Finally Nick makes a few passes,
pausing in front of the dog. This makes a charming
picture, and I take a photo of Nick looking at
Brown-dog.

No net boats come in, so no fish. At 7:50 I go in
for breakfast. At 8:30, no dolphins are in sight.
Fishermen are cleaning nets and throwing fish to
the gulls. They say, "No dolphins came in today."
(They hadn't seen the sunrise contingent.) Finally I
spot Holey-fin and Joy way off to the left, but they
are paying no attention to the fishing boats'
dispensation. Still windy, but bright sun. At 11:00
several dolphins are attracted by a middle aged
couple who say they've come here for the day
especially to see dolphins, having been told about
them by a friend who'd been here earlier this year.
The man stands on shore in his shoes with a camera
while the lady stays calf deep in the water for a
longer and longer period, perhaps forty minutes,

unable to tear herself away. Nick and Puck
especially come to her, singly or together, with
open mouths. "Oh, it let me touch its beak! . . . oh,
it let me pat its head!" She learns to chuck it under
the chin. I am stroking Nick and Holey-fin along
their sides. The brown dog is here too, standing
eagerly up to his belly in the water. Two little boys
are also engaging with the dolphins. They try
several times to touch the dolphins' big fins, and
each time, the animals startle and swish away
quickly.

Some bits of mangled fish are offered. The
dolphin accepts a piece politely ("Oh, look, he took
it. Did you get that?" "Yes, I got the picture."), but
then drops it in the water. The lady retrieves it and
offers it again. It is quite interesting to me how
often this occurs, that the dolphins will continue to
accept into their mouths whatever is offered, taking
it with sweet grace, and then just turn away and
drop it; and the humans seem to be oblivious of
what that might mean: that the dolphins don't
want what is offered! Nick and Holey each take
again something they have already dropped twice
before finally refusing it, and Puck and Crooked-fin
once each.

I spend more than an hour, not offering
anything except stroking and talking. The faithful
five are there off and on, with Nick most close.
Three to five others are lolling around far out, and
the ones in close go off to the left to see what is
happening with the boats, or go out deeper to laze
around, and then come back. Today there is another
familiar-looking dolphin that I think, from my
memory of last year, may be "Beautiful."

Sometimes the games offshore get very active,
with one dolphin apparently being pursued by one
or two others in a fast chase, ending in leaps and
tumbles. Even with binoculars I cannot identify

any of them when they are playing, because they are
above the water so briefly, and moving so fast. Only
baby Joy is obvious, because she is so much smaller.
She leaps out of the water fairly often, once every
half-hour or so.

After a little time out deep they usually come
back. At least one or two are with us all the time.
Tony Ingham, who runs the little fast food shop in
Denham is here with me, having come to exchange
some talk about our yoga experiences. I discussed
with him the possibilities of contacting the
dolphins through meditation. Now he stays mostly
at the water's edge being with the dolphins more
inwardly.

It is a sunny day but with a chilling wind, tide
getting low. Once when all the dolphins wander off,
I try calling them back by striking two stones
together underwater, and one of the boys joins me.
Nick comes to investigate. I say to him, "Talk to
me, Nick. I've never heard you talk." Wilf had
insisted that Nick speaks to him, and I wanted to
hear it. Nick is doing his routine thing of coming to
within inches of my knees, lifting open a beak,
tolerating a stroke on top of the beak or under the
chin or along his side as he turns away, swimming
off for a minute or two, and then returning for the
same. I make a chucking noise, as one makes to a
horse, and say again several times, "Come on, Nick,
talk to me." He takes a turn with one eye out of the

water, looking at me. Finally, as he approaches, I
heart a soft squealing sound. He did it! It was so quiet
a sound that I might easily have missed it if I hadn't
been listening intently. Perhaps they *have* been
talking to me all along. How is it done? Not with the
blow-hole, as I was looking right at it. He'd already
done his quick puff-and-gasp breath, and the
blow-hole cover was quite still. Anyway, I am
thrilled. I ask the boy if he's ever heard them do that,
and he says he has, a few times.

Tide is getting low. About 2:30 Tony leaves,
and I go to my caravan to write.

I return to the beach about 4:30. None in sight,
even far out. Tide very low, with the paler water
showing where the sandbank is, about a kilometer
offshore. I walk off west along the beach for an hour
and a half with the Mason's dog, Pluto, as company,
picking shells. The tide is extremely low and just
turns at sunset. Still no dolphins are in sight, as
darkness comes.

I am reading *Follow a Wild Dolphin* by Horace
Dobbs; I note that little is really known of the
"social behavior" of wild bottlenosed dolphins.
This would be the ideal place to learn something of
that. But could it be done without disrupting them?
Hazel and Wilf are concerned that there be no
interference with the dolphins' lives, and surely
that would be essential: not to interfere so much
that behavior is changed. But of course their lives
here are already not "natural" (in the sense of an
"ordinary dolphin life), in that they have chosen to
have this contact with people. Because of that they
are fed some food that they then don't have to catch
for themselves (and we don't know if this is enough
food to have any effect on them), and they spend
time just "hanging out" with us humans, which
may have some effect on their relations with each
other.

Wilf and I talk about how we humans have altered our environment so much for so many generations that we are now dependent upon our shelter and clothing, for example, for our very survival. If exposed to the cold wind and rain without roof and clothing, we will literally die. Or even if exposed to the hot sun without clothing, our skin may be so burned that we perish. Wilf has a fair complexion that burns so readily in the hot sun that he must wear a hat, and keep a shirt covering his shoulders and back. We are actually now dependent on all the "things" that we have made with our clever hands and brains just to keep ourselves alive. I remembered the studies of gorillas I had seen in the marvelous BBC film series *Life on Earth*. Gorillas are so strong that they have no enemies, and their food of green growing vegetation is plentiful, so they have a very easy, happy life, with no work to speak of. Just pick a green shoot and eat it. Lie around and groom one another. Play-wrestle.

Likewise the dolphin. Catch a fish and swallow. Swim around with your mates (Australian use of that word, meaning "buddies"), leap and roll and play. Go see what's up. An easy, happy, joyful life. Boring? That's our problem, isn't it? We can't imagine having it all that easy. No problems to solve? No possessions to look after? No responsibilities? We can scarcely imagine it.

On this evening I practiced some meditation, using the idea or concept of "dolphin" as a sort of mantra or mandala. I'll describe exactly what I did: After doing a little stretching, keeping attention intently in the body, I relaxed briefly, keeping attention focused in sensation of muscles and tissues, now feeling relaxed. Then I sat in half-lotus, with spine erect and balanced, and did some long-tone chanting "OOOMMM, OOOMMM,OOOMMM" in a deep, vibrant voice, as is my custom, feeling the vibrations of the sound in the body. Sitting quietly erect, allowing the vibrations to flow away slowly, I began to focus attention on the presence of the concept of "dolphin." I suppose I had both the word and the picture of dolphin in my mind, but mostly it was just the beingness of dolphin that gradually filled my consciousness, so that no other awareness was present. There was no sensation of time passing, or of anything "happening." It was just a very great space, infinitely large, infinitely silent, going on forever in time — infinitely beautiful to be there. I have had similar experiences often before in meditation, and it is hard to say in what way this particular meditation was connected with dolphin-ness, but it was. By actual clock, I suppose this went on for only about twenty minutes. Toward the end there was more experience of sensation and happening — a sense of being in the sea, of dolphin-like breath, of powerful, lithe muscular body, of glorious excitement. Then I returned my awareness somewhat reluctantly to my own human body, feeling very deeply and quietly joyful. There I was in my little caravan, with moonlight coming in the window, and time for evening meal. All very prosaic and pleasant. What was the "message"? Well, none in words. Just a fine feeling. Just, isn't it nice to *be*!

Sunday 24 August 80

At 5:10 I awake to see the nearly full moon setting, a lovely sight. Very windy, with the caravan shaken by gusts, but not very cold. Not yet dawn, so I doze again. In wakening fully a little later, I am aware of the squeaky chirp of the welcome swallow, the friendly little common swallow of these parts, and think how similar it is to the squeaky chirpy sound of the dolphin.

At sunrise I go out, but see no dolphins. Still very windy, but steady now. I go back to read and write, and at 10:30 go out again. A group of adults and children are at water's edge. The tide is high, and Holey-fin is nose-in at their feet, looking very large, with little Joy cavorting behind her. (How large is Holey-fin? About two-and-a-half meters long, I would judge.)

"Isn't it lovely!," and similar comments, as cameras snap. "Don't get your cardigan wet," one mother says to her nine-year-old daughter, but the child's delighted face doesn't register the admonition as she raptly watches Holey-fin turn and pass and turn again. Clothing can be dried. I wade in and show the children how to stroke the

dolphin under the beak and along the side. No one
has any fish, and the dolphin is content just to pass
and repass the row of little legs in the water, with
occasional touching of little hands. Brown-dog is
there also, of course. Soon Holey-fin drifts away
deeper, and then Nick appears. As usual he makes
one pass with an eye out of the water, surveying the
scene. Then he noses in and lifts his open beak out
of the water at my knees. I greet him, "Hello, Nick,"
and stroke the top of his beak. He pushes against my
hand, and I laughingly give the hard rubbery beak a
good rub. He stays long enough for the eager boy
next to me to also give him a pat. Soon four children
are touching him each time he comes by. When he
swishes his tail to move away, they jerk back in
fright, but I keep soothing them, "He won't hurt
you. He's a very gentle creature," and they grow
more confident. Holey-fin comes back for more too.
I explain that she is mother of baby Joy, and also of
Nick, aged four-and-a-half.

One woman tells me that she and her husband
and children had come by one day last year while on
holiday up here from Perth, but there had not
been any dolphins in sight and they were so
disappointed. Now they are happy. It was worth
another two-hour drive all the way off the main
highway, she says, delighted with the experience.

Nick is being especially attentive to me, and I
am able to give him long palm strokes along his
side. After half-an-hour of this, interspersed with
quick dashes out to deep water, and an occasional
glide by with eye out of the water to look, he begins
to come in very slowly and hold almost still, while I
and the children gently stroke his side with a flat
palm. He seems to like that better than fingers.
Meanwhile the children's parents are happily
clicking their cameras from the beach. Twice Nick
leans against my leg as I stroke him and say a few

times, "Talk to me, Nick," and then he does, twice,
his soft little squealing sound, as he passes, with my
hand pressed against his side. Then Holey-fin does
it too.

An older couple come down to the beach with a
packet of fish to feed the dolphins. (Hazel sells them
from her freezer, 50 cents for five fish.) This gives a
whole different mood to things. The woman wades
out with fish in hand and waits while her husband
gets the camera ready, Nick lifting his whole head
out, eager for the fish. He gets it. Then one for
Holey-fin.

She gives one fish to a boy to feed, and Nick
takes it and bites the head off, then goes around in
the water for a while with the fish in his mouth. I
say, "Nick, you're not very hungry, are you?" I reach
my hand toward him, and he brings the fish,
hanging crosswise in his mouth, and lays it in my
hand. Then, when I offer it to him turned straight,
he swallows it. I'm not sure what that is all about.

Next the lady takes a fish in each hand and tries
to get Nick to take one and Holey-fin the other at
the same time, while the man waits to photograph.
Her attention is more on the camera than on the
dolphins, and it isn't working out very well.
Brown-dog gets in the way, and then Nick, coming
in sideways, blocks Holey-fin, so finally the lady
gives up and feeds first Nick and then Holey-fin.

After that we can't really pet them any more.
There are no more fish, and although I'm sure they
aren't that hungry (there are plenty of fish in the
sea!), when I reach to stroke Nick again, twice he
snaps his jaws together irritably. There is not that
loving spirit anymore, but a sense of crossness. I
almost wonder if he might actually snap my fingers,
although I'm quite sure he wouldn't. I don't really
like feeding them.

No other dolphins in sight, just the three:

Holey-fin and her two children, little Joy and
adolescent Nick, who continues to entertain
another group of visitors when I look again at 12:30.

At 2:30 the dolphins are gone, the tide is lower,
the sun is hot, and a strong, steady breeze blows
from the southeast. A man cleaning fish at water's
edge feeds the gulls, but no dolphins are in sight,
even far out. The tide is very low until sunset when
the moon rises, almost full, but no more dolphins.
The tides are sometimes strange here at Monkey
Mia — only one change in 24 hours on some days.

Monday 25 August

Very windy clear dawn. Sea very choppy and
chilly. At 8:15 there are many dolphins all crowding
in to shore where there is the usual group: children
knee-deep in the water, with parents and
grandparents on shore with cameras. Fishermen

cleaning their nets throw an occasional fish out
over the heads of the crowd, to dolphins not very
interested. Probably the dolphins had fed
themselves quite well today out in the bay. They are
being very active, chasing each other, rolling over
one another lengthwise, and turning belly-up to
glide upside down. They come in just to see the
people, beak out to be touched by delighted
children, or glide by slowly with one wise eye
observing. There are many today! — and all very
close in high tide. They look so large when they are
within one meter of water's edge. It is difficult to
count them when they are so active and romping
together, tails and fins appearing and disappearing
all mixed up together, but there are at least eight.
The best way is to try to identify each one. Here is
Holey-fin and little Joy — that is easy. And of
course Nick. Today he swims by with eye above
water, recognizes me, and noses right in to my
knees and waits with head submerged for a long
stroke along his side. I am pleased he is not looking
for a fish. He gets several strokes as he turns and
returns, and a pet on the beak.

Hey, here's a new one, who comes right up to
my knees, lifts its head and accepts a pat on the
beak at first meeting! It looks a bit larger than Nick
and Puck, an adolescent. Could it be Beautiful's
baby, now a four-and-a-half year old? I look hard for
marks on its fin or head, trying to keep track of this
dolphin in the milling playing mob. No, I have lost
it, but I don't think there are any marks. Here is
Puck now, and Crooked-fin. Nick comes again and
again for strokes, and once when I am stroking
another dolphin, Nick takes my toes in his teeth!
Not hard, just a pinch, but what a surprise!

And here is the large dolphin that was here
Saturday, that I thought might be Beautiful. She has
a squiggle of deep dark scars on her head, shaped

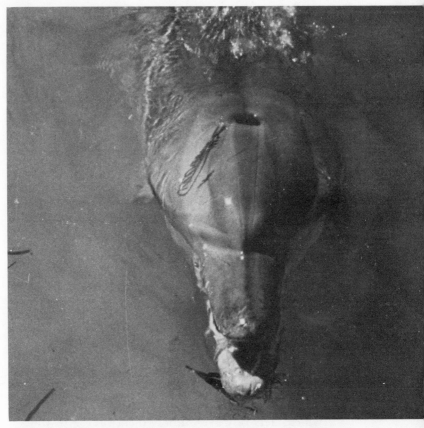

like a feather, and two very small bits missing from
the trailing edge of her dorsal fin. She is as long as
Holey and Crooked-fin, and seems larger in girth at
about the area of the flippers. There is another one
whose fin is somewhat sickle-shaped with no nicks
or notches. I don't believe this one has been in to
touch, but I am not sure. They are so active today!
There are at least eight. I have gotten soaked to the
waist in the choppy water.

    Something special occurs when the adolescent
one (later identified for me by Wilf as being
Beautiful's baby, or "B.B.") comes in and holds still,
head lifted with mouth slightly open, facing
straight towards me. There is this strong *stillness* in

my mind . . . a kind of joyful peace. After it ducks
under and swishes away, I realize again that I forgot
to look for marks. I seem to go blank when this one
is here and I am touching it.

The large one with the feather-shaped scar also
comes to me several times to be patted on the beak,
and each I feel she is saying, "Oh, hello. You are
back for another visit. Good to see you." I definitely
feel that she recognizes me, and must have been
here last year. Yes, I am sure it is Beautiful.

The other dolphins that have been chasing one
another up and down, now come back, and there is
general turmoil. One little boy wants to go in
swimming with them. He puts on a mask and
swims out. At once they all retreat to at least five
meters distance, and keep away from him. He gives
up and comes back to stand with us, but with the
mask still on his face. No dolphins come near us. I
suggest that he take the mask off, as they do not
seem to like it. So he removes it, and they return
one by one. They tolerate him splashing around
among them, but not letting him touch them,
much as they tolerate Brown-dog (who is here as
always). The boy asks me "Would they give me a
ride?" "I don't know, they might. You could try to
grasp a fin and see." But his approach is too sudden.
He stands until one is near, then throws himself in
the water grasping for the dorsal fin, and each time
the dolphin is gone in a flash. Soon they have all
gone out five meters to play their own games,
chasing and rolling and diving.

As they speed back and forth they go under the
pier off to the right, and some adolescent boys are
throwing crab spears down from there. Concerned
that a dolphin might be struck by a spear, I go in to
see if Wilf wants to talk to them about it. He is away
in town, but Hazel asks me to mind the store while
she goes. She tells them to be very careful not to

throw anything if the dolphins are swimming under the pier. "If you hurt one of them, our dolphins might not come in any more."

I am cold, and go inside to get dry, but come back out about 10:30. A new family is on the shore, enraptured. "Aren't they beautiful. We're staying in Denham and just heard about them last night. We wouldn't have missed this for anything."

Three dolphins, Beautiful with her feather mark, Sickle-fin, and the young one I think is B.B., are close in, and Holey-fin and Joy and others are farther out. The man and boy say they have noticed one has a small wound on the head that was bleeding. We look carefully at those who come close, but evidently it was only small and stopped bleeding. I look at the boys on the pier, who are now out at the end, fishing. I do not really believe they would have deliberately hurt the dolphin. Perhaps these energetic creatures injure themselves playing. They do seem to have many scars, and are very rough today — wild, free and joyful. A very exhilarating windy day.

Hazel tells me, "Beautiful's baby is back. When I went out to speak to the boys, she came right to me. You know she disappeared for months, and we felt sure we saw her that day three weeks ago when there were 15 here. Before she went away, every time I fed her she would look at me in that special way, and I felt she was trying to tell me something. I would try to make my mind a blank, to receive the message, but I just couldn't seem to get whatever it was.

"I remember a man who came one day, an older man near 60, who came in the shop and asked to buy dolphin food, and I gave him some fish. His manner was very skeptical, almost scornful, and he walked out very offhand. After a while he came back, and he looked so different! His eyes,

especially, were kind of changed. He hung around
with a far-off look and waited until no one else was
in the shop, then looked around outside. He leaned
over the counter and said softly, very serious, "You
know, those dolphins — one of them . . .," he
glanced over his shoulder again, "Well I hope you
don't think I'm crazy, but . . . I think it's trying to
tell me something." I said, "Yes, I know what you
mean. I often think it's trying to tell *me* something.
But I don't know what it is. What do you think?"
And we just looked at each other.

Well, me too. What is it? Maybe it is
just . . . love . . . .

It is interesting to note that Hazel called this
dolphin "she." We don't know the sex of any of the
dolphins here except the three mothers, Holey-fin
Crooked-fin, and Beautiful, because they have been
seen suckling their young. But we tend to call Nick
"he," partly because that name in human use is
usually short for Nicholas, a male name. But

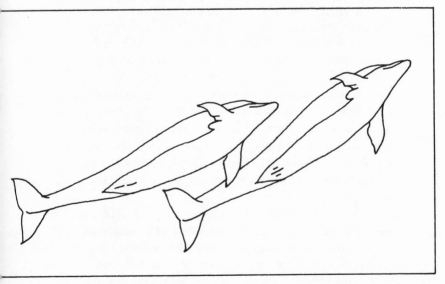

actually in this case the dolphin is called that
because of a very prominent "nick" in the top of the
fin, and may not be a male dolphin. We have come
to think of the new baby as a female because its
name is "Joy," a feminine name among humans, but
in this case the dolphin is called that simply
because we experience such joy in watching the
dear little thing. We cannot tell the sex of these
dolphins because the genital organs are inside
tightly closed slits in the streamlined body. If we
could get a good look at the underside, we could tell
by the arrangement of the slits, because females
have slits for a pair of teats. But these dolphins will
not allow us to be near them with a face mask on, so
we have never been able to get a good look under
water!

1:00. The games are still going on. On shore is a
group of holiday-makers to entertain and be
entertained. The trio of unfamiliar dolphins that I
had noticed earlier are the only ones right here at
the moment. They swim in very close formation
about three meters out, back and forth, and only
one keeps veering off to nose in where there are
human legs in the water. Of the two who do not
come near, one has a large distinctly sickle-shaped
fin, and the other has a fin with a very small slice
out of the back edge. I can't see their heads or tails
well enough to see if there are any marks there. The
one who comes in may be our "message" dolphin of
a while ago. (It has fine parallel white lines across
the top where neck creases might be.) They
continue their close "trio" movements, with the
one leaving the others to come close, again and
again. When some fish are brought, Nick and Puck,
Holey-fin and Beautiful appear also. Lots of action.
Tide still quite deep.

3:00. Tide lower now. Only Holey-fin, Joy and
Nick are left. Nick still comes to anyone wading

into the water. How many hours today has he been
here?! Brown-dog, too.

At 4:30, an occasional dolphin arches above
water taking a breath, but far out. By 5:00 all are
gone, the bay empty of its playful invaders.

Tuesday 26 August 80

At pre-dawn there is a steady blow, something
flapping outside the caravan. At 6:00 my hopes for a
view of the full moon setting at dawn are dashed, as
my ears come into consciousness to the sound of
light rain. I go out to the loo, and walk down to the
beach in a drizzle. The sea is very still at half-tide.
Yes, one large fin about three meters out, makes its
appearance with the breathing slow arch, a good big
fin with no marks obvious at this distance in this
light. It could be Crooked-fin, who has the biggest
fin of all the familiars. The rain increases, so I go
back to bed for another half-four, which seems the
best thing to do on such a morning.

At 8:30 the drizzle has stopped. The air is still,
and not cold. There is high overcast. Sea half out
and very still. A group of children knee-deep in the
water are petting several dolphins, but by the time I
join them there are only Nick and Puck, who pass
and turn and pass, approach, hold, turn, pass
allowing brief touching now and then. I love the
way they tilt to one side on a slow glide, lifting one
wise old eye out of the water to view the airy world,
then back under to the watery world. The eye has a
lid (unlike most water creatures) and seems quite
expressive — wise, mischievous, merry, lovingly
gentle. One wonders exactly what it is about an eye
that creates expression — the degree of openness,
tiny wrinkles this way or that of tissue around the
eye. I remember once studying closely the way that
Charles Schulz gives a great variety of expression to
the face of the cartoon dog, Snoopy, by the tiniest

change of line of the eyes. But it does seem that there is more to eye expression than just the changes of tissue around it. When we gaze into an eye we may have a strong impression of being shut "out," or of being allowed "in," of seeing into the inner being. Of being *seen* into. Gazing into a dog's eyes we may sense the typical canine adoration, or the intelligent understanding of the meaning of what we are saying. In the eyes of a child we may see the trust ... or the doubt. Is it possible that all we see is subjective? Do we see emotions in another that we merely create out of our own emotions and expectations? However it may be, to be observed by a dolphin's eye is a rare experience. He seems to just *see*, and to accept it all. I recall a famous Indian teacher of Vipassana meditation who would listen to a student tell of his difficulties with continued hour upon hour of meditation and so many troubling things going through the mind, and the teacher would merely answer, "Observe, observe." See it all, accept it all. Everything just is. "Being only is."

This is the sense I get from the dolphin's eye. "I see it all, I understand it all, it all *is*." But also, "It all is ... *interesting*!!!!" That is the dolphin zest!

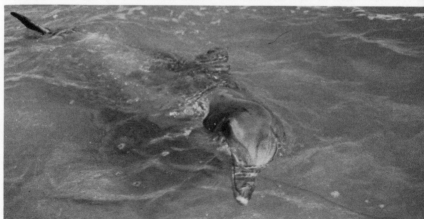

This grey quiet morning, I stand for an hour, calf to knee-deep in the chilly water. Holey-fin and little Joy come in, and disappear. Then Crooked-fin. Some dolphins are lingering near the boats (no nets with fish), while others are with us near the "jetty" (as it is called in Australia, "pier" to us in America.)

Brown-dog is here too, of course, up to his shoulders in water, watching, watching eager and patient. I learn that the dog's name is "Ringer," and he belongs to a family here for a long fishing holiday.

Occasionally I see a dog come here and bark at the dolphins. I can imagine how they must seem to the ordinary dog, especially when the children of *his* family wade out there among these big strange animals who approach the children with mouths open, out there in the water where he cannot protect them very effectively. It seems natural that he would bark.

Once I saw a dog go into the water and try to nip at the dolphins. What did they do? They easily swam out of reach, looking at him. Then he quieted down and gazed after them, and later watched them intently from shore. It is rather odd, actually, that more dogs do not react by barking. If a dog persists in barking, the Masons require the owners to keep it tied, but they say this rarely occurs. Most dogs watch the dolphins in a slightly puzzled way from time to time and then ignore them. But this one dog, Ringer, has developed a fine fascination for them. He is spellbound.

On this particular day, the children tire and leave, except for one little girl. Of all the dolphins, only Puck is still here, gliding and turning. He passes quite close by Ringer several times, slowly, almost brushing his feet. Ringer seems to hold his breath. Is that joy in the dog's eyes? It seems so. The dolphin keeps his head under water, as if nosing the dog's feet, then slowly turns, and glides on by. Three times he does this, while the dog shifts eagerly between passes, but stays very still while the dolphin is close. What is passing between them? Do they have a communication we don't know of?

Today I notice that Nick has two short deep
cuts on the right side of the face. Later, in the shop, I
ask Hazel and Wilf, "Do you think they bite each
other in play, as puppies and kittens do? But as
fiercely as kittens bite in wrestling, I've never seen
them actually draw blood. Might the dolphins do
that? They were playing very wildly yesterday."
"We really don't know. Perhaps they get scratched
on rocks while going after fish. Or on barnacles
under the jetty. They do have many scars, don't
they? The fins especially."

   "It seems strange, doesn't it," I said, "that they
get hurt so much when they have such good sonar,
or whatever it is that lets them know where
everything is located. I've seen them swim *so fast*,
so close to boats and things, just avoiding scraping
by a hair's breadth. How could they mistake, and get
cut? . . . It's a mystery." These cuts could not be
from biting each other. Their teeth are close
together and all the same length, so a bite would
make a whole row of scars.

At 10:30 the tide is all the way in. The usual children and camera-laden adults are offering dead fish to Holey-fin and Nick, with little Joy cavorting in the water behind them. No others are in sight. It is interesting that Holey-fin and her two offspring *always* seem to be here during the day except when the tide gets too shallow.

An older couple tell me of when they were here years ago. "How many years?" "Oh, mebbe 11. And the dolphins would snag it off!" (I find I really doubt this story. Why do I believe so much in the dolphins' good will?) "Would they let you touch them then, as they do now?" "I dunno. We never tried. There was this one who had part of his tail shot off. He used to help get fish into the nets sometimes. They had a name for him, Charley I think it was. But one day they found him dead on the rocks. Probably somebody killed him." I'd heard a number of stories about old Charley, but not about part of his tail being missing.

At noon they are still there. Nick and Puck remind me of two rather rowdy adolescents. They spend many hours a day together, and clearly have a very close bond. They often coast along quietly side by side in synchronized breathing, sharing a warm moment, then suddenly one will break away and race ahead, and the other tears off following. Usually Nick, who is the older, leads, but sometimes it is Puck who takes off like a streak, and Nick gives chase. Then a rough and tumble game ensues, with flukes and beaks and fins in all directions as they roll over one another and leap and duck and dive. Sometimes, as with most adolescents who have grown up together, they shove one another away at feeding time, or when we are stroking them. Nick usually wins, as he is a little bigger and more aggressive. Sometimes I feel cross with the little hellions with all their splashing and jostling.

Today when Nick shoves against Holey-fin she slaps the water sharply with her tail and follows him with her steady eye, and he immediately becomes better behaved. Once Crooked-fin clacks her jaws at the two boisterous young dolphins, and they take their energetic games out to deeper water. Some time later they return to us in a much quieter mood and are quite disarmingly sweet and endearing. How can I help but love them, as they both approach me gently and each nuzzles his beak into my hand. Oh, you sweethearts. My heart

melts. They move on past me together, each leaning against one of my hands in passing, to get long strokes along their sides.

In the shop Hazel remarks about the crowd at the beach. She could see their backs from her place

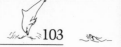

behind the counter in the store. "Must be dolphins there." "Yes," I say, "they're there." I've just come back from watching again — Nick, Puck, and their two mothers, Holey-fin and Crooked-fin, and baby Joy — the usuals. I buy a pencil with a rubber cap on it in the shape of a dolphin leaping out of an ocean wave. The Masons have just received an enlargement of a beautiful photo of one of the dolphins close-up, with the sun glistening off the wet skin, making a perfect star right on its forehead. Just as I've seen them many times.

I spent much of the afternoon in my caravan meditating. I'd thought of sitting on the beach or on the pier, close to the dolphins, to "tune in" to them, but there was too much comotion there. Also, I never like to be conspicuous when I meditate. I decided I'd be able to "tune in" to the dolphins if I were 100 meters back just as well as from three. No matter where I am, it is lovely being with them in consciousness. It's a sense of beingness, a fine contentment, a watery wordlessness, an intense awareness. If there is a message, it seems to be, "Look, you don't need all this *stuff.*" A message on the *simplicity* of joy.

At 2:00 the tide is going out. I see mother and baby gliding along together, so closely that it seems baby is suckling. They turn and glide and turn again, baby half behind, very close and half under, with its white belly showing a little, surely suckling. Then I realize . . . that isn't Holey-fin. That's Crooked-fin! No hole and jagged edge in the fin, and definitely a strong curve over at the top of the fin when seen from head on. Then, is she nursing little Joy? Does she serve as a sort of foster-mum at times? I've seen several different dolphins romping with little Joy, the favorite little sister of the whole clan. But feeding? Is that possible? Or is it really not Joy, but Puck —

Crooked-fin's own offspring, now three-and-a-half
years old? Could he be still feeding from his mum?
This baby certainly does not look big enough to be
Puck. They swim off into deep water before I can
tell absolutely, but I feel sure it is Joy. A mystery.
Observing dolphins that are so active and free to
come and go as these are in such a wide space is a
very tricky business.

At 6:00 the sun is almost ready to set, and the
tide has gone quite low. But they are still here!
There are four or five children and an adult or two in
the water and others on shore with cameras. It has
gone on all day — Holey-fin and Nick and Puck,
with Crooked-fin coming in occasionally. It is
necessary now to wade far out into the mucky mud,
but these newly arrived children do not mind, so
pleased are they to see the pet dolphins. One little
girl, about nine years old, turns her radiant face to
me as I wade out. "We fed them fish, and they let us
touch them. Aren't they beautiful?" she gasps.
Beautiful . . . the word so many use, a beautiful
experience. "They'd let you touch them even if you
didn't give them fish," I explain to her. "Really?"
She looks intrigued but skeptical. "I touch them all
the time, and I almost never feed them. Look." The
fish are all gone, but the dolphins glide back and
forth tirelessly, occasionally nosing in for a pat on
the beak. The child is delighted, as are the others
present.

I'd really like to see this feeding routine
dropped. Imagine how many fish have been given
today, hour after hour. Nick still comes with open
mouth and takes whatever is offered, even if it is
mangled bits of fish, or frozen and not thawed. Half
the time he turns and drops it. But even if it is
dragged out of the water and offered to him again, he
will take it again. On the other hand, he will come
again and again and again to have me run my palm

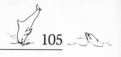

down his side in a long stroke. He leans his weight against my hand and makes his soft little squealing sound, as if to say "Mmmmmmmmmmm" with pleasure.

Guess who else has never quit during this whole long day of about ten hours: the brown dog, Ringer. Here he is out in this cold mucky water, swimming a little because his feet barely touch and the very slight lift of surf makes him lose his footing at times, shivering as the sun goes down, but absolutely rapt. When Nick or Puck or Holey-fin comes near him, he holds perfectly still, allowing them to nudge him or pass him by, as he watches adoringly. I wonder how he will be when he is taken home again, wherever that is . . . Will he pine for them? Will he have doggy dreams of dolphins? Are they pouring blessed dolphin consciousness all over him, as they are over us?

In the evening I was reading an article in
National Geographic, April 1979, "The Trouble
with Dolphins." Dolphins and tuna feed on the
same small fish, so when tuna boats sight dolphins,
they follow them and are led to vast schools of tuna,
where they then put out their enormous nets,
catching both tuna and dolphins. They used to kill
all the dolphins caught in the nets, by the
thousands. But due to public uproar, government
regulation, and some realization on the part of the
fisheries that if all the dolphins were gone they
could no longer lead them to the tuna, this practice
is being somewhat abated. The regulatory goal set
for 1978 was to reduce dolphin deaths to 52,000, but
what actually happened was that "only" 15,000,
died — at least according to someone's count. That
is good, and due, of course, to lots of energy on the
part of protesters (in California I don't buy canned
tuna, as a protest to dolphin killing), as well as a
modicum of common sense on the part of the
fishers. But heavens!, fifteen thousand! If they were
human beings, what would happen if even one were
killed?

But then, I don't know. I've also been reading in
Capricornia, by Xavier Herberts, some passages
about how aborigines were massacred here in
Australia in the early years. The native people of
America recall similar events in our own history.
So, being *homo sapiens* is no protection. If those
dolphins were humans who just happened to be
sea-dwelling, that would be enough difference from
"us" to make the fishers, and those who use their
products, feel it is acceptable to slaughter a mere
15,000 a year in order to have convenient cans of
tuna fish to make into sandwiches or to dump into a
quick casserole or salad. At least we are not eating
the dolphins, or at least not that I know of.

But of course, dolphins eat fish. Everybody eats

somebody in this old world, even if it is only a blade of grass. Maybe man has more obsession with death and suffering because we have been so involved with it other than for eating. It is all a puzzle. Most animals do not seem all that concerned about suffering. And death is something that happens, though to be avoided if possible. (Nick seems totally unconcerned about the new cuts on his face.) Do we anthropomorphize too much about suffering and death in animals, when *we* are the ones who so often inflict suffering needlessly?

In a more pleasant vein, there was another article in this issue of *National Geographic* about a dolphin in the Bahamas that makes friends with scuba divers. Apparently a number of divers have had this dolphin approach them underwater, have played with him, and then met him again on another day to play again. He is called Sandy and is identified by natural fin and fluke marks, as we identify our dolphins. It is perhaps odd that the dolphins here at Monkey Mia will not let us swim with them, and especially not let anyone dive with them.

During this week I also read Horace Dobbs beautiful book *Follow a Wild Dolphin*, about his dolphin friend, Donald. Dobbs and a woman friend met Donald while diving off Great Britain, and enjoyed his repeated visits for some weeks. Then he disappeared. Quite some time later, Dobbs heard of a friendly dolphin in another location, and went to see it, only to find that it was Donald again. After a number of weeks of friendly play, the dolphin again disappeared. But once more, upon traveling to investigate reports of yet another unusual dolphin, Dobbs found that this dolphin, too, was Donald.

This was an enormous dolphin, some six meters long, more than twice the size of ours. To meet such an animal in deep water must be a bit

scary, and it is fascinating to read of how the divers
learned to experience his gentle playfulness. How
many humans have missed wonderful meetings
with our fellow creatures because we were afraid?

Wednesday 27 August 80

6:00. Silvery full moon at dawn sinking in a sky
tinted rose to indigo to lemon. Windy. Tide fairly
low. No dolphins in sight.

8:30. A crowd gathers at water's edge as usual
— children standing in the water with two or three
adults, other adults on the sand with cameras, or
holding babies, or handing fish to those in the
water. It is remarkable to see, even after witnessing
it over and over, day after day, how the dolphins
come right in among the people. One might expect,
for example, that they would want to make sure, in
approaching someone standing in the water, that no
one else was in the water behind them to cut off
their escape to the sea, perhaps. But of course, no
one here has ever tried to pen them in.

Here they are, wriggling right up into the
shallow water to get a fish from a shy small child,
while larger children stand in the deeper water
behind them patting the beaks of other dolphins. At
one point three big dolphins are in-shore of the
children standing deeper, and the whole crowd of
five dolphins and nine humans are all jammed
together in a space the size of an ordinary living
room, say four by five meters, and in water only
knee-deep to those farthest out, which means the
dolphins' bellies are scraping bottom. They are not
still, though, for more than a few seconds at a time,
weaving and wriggling and gliding in and out,
suddenly giving a strong sideways swish of their
powerful body and then an upward stroke of the
tail, and out to water a half-meter deep to glide back
and forth a few times. Then in among the crowd

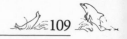

again, lifting an open beak to take a fish, or just to be petted.

A little boy, Kim, who is a great dolphin lover, is staying for some time here at the caravan park. He says, "Oh, some have already left. But there is Holey-fin. And here is Puck. And there is Nick. And there's little Joy with Crooked-fin, just out there." "Is she playing nanny today?" I suggest. He laughs. "Yes, she must be."

Holey-fin and Crooked-fin seem often to share responsibilities for their youngsters, much as human mothers might. "I need some exercise. Will you watch the baby while I go for a brisk swim?" "Of course." So Holey goes off and leaps and plays with the other dolphins in deep water while Crooked-fin stays near little Joy. Either mother may occasionally give a quick disciplinary slap or jaw-clack to their two adolescents when they

become very rowdy. Last year Crooked-fin was the
mother of the youngest dolphin. Her Puck was still
quite small. Then Beautiful used to join more in the
sisterly child-care arrangement, but now she is not
here as frequently.

All the regulars are here. And about six meters
out, the occasional dark fin and back appear in the
breathing surface-and-arch-and-dive slow tumble
they do. Kim's eyes shine as he talks about them.
"The kids at school won't believe me when I tell
them I petted wild dolphins every day." "Will you
have some photographs to show them?" I ask. "Yes,
my dad took some. When they see those, they'll
have to believe me, won't they? "Yes, they will. Tell
me, what do you like about the dolphins?" "What do
I *like* about them?" He looks at me in
astonishment, as if to say, "*You* should know. We've
met in the water every day." Then he tries to
articulate it. "Well, I dunno, they're just so friendly.
They feel so good to touch. Their skin is so smooth.
It feels nice to be here with them. I feel like the dog,
you know," he chuckles, ruffling Ringer's woolly
neck. "I just feel happy, being here with them."

"When you get back to school, will you write
about them for a school paper?" I ask him.

"Yeah," he says. "We always have to write about
what we did for school holidays. I can write a *lot*
about them. I bet I could write about five pages!"

I'd love to see what he writes. Will these
children's lives be influenced by this contact with
the dolphins? A father watching his children
stroking the dolphins tells me that they live in
Perth. "We're just taking the two weeks, you know,
the school holidays, to drive around up here in the
northwest, let the children have all these
experiences. My mum and dad, now, they're old.
They tell us, go and see it all while you're young,
while you can get around. They're in their seventies

now, and Mum, she's got arthritis. They can't go
much. But these kids, now, they're having a
marvelous time. Look at that. My boy, he's having a
fine time with that dolphin!"

At first the children are wary. The dolphins
come so close, and their bodies *are* big: Nick and
Puck about two meters long, and the full grown
ones a good two-and-a-half meters with strong
heavy bodies, a mass of muscle. The little teeth
look very sharp when they open their mouths,
though I've never seen them close down on
anybody. Then, of course, those dorsal fins coming
through the water! Often I hear comments from the
children about sharks. They have all been heavily
conditioned about the terror of sharks, and a
triangular fin just showing above the water is the
symbol of horrible death in the teeth of a giant
shark. Apparently every Australian child has seen
the movie *Jaws* (I have not seen it, and do not intend
to do so), and is terrified at the very idea of a shark.
One mother even says, "The children are getting so
trusting now, with these dolphins playing here, that
they're probably not even going to get out of the
water if they see a real shark later on."

I suggest that sharks rarely bother people. She
says, "Oh they do where we live, near Perth." I say,
"The probablities are much greater of being badly
injured in an automobile than by a shark, but you do
not teach your children to be terrified every time
they get in the car. You don't need to teach them to
be afraid in the water." "Well, that's true," she says
musingly. One little girl says while stroking the
dolphin along its side, "I thought its skin would be
rough like a shark" (she had touched a dead shark),
"but it's lovely and smooth." "Why would it be
anything like a shark? It isn't related to a shark at
all." "Isn't it?" she asks. "It looks rather like a
shark." "Do you think so?" I ask. "You mean

because of the big fin?" "Yes, I guess so,"
shuddering. "You know, it's really much more
closely related to *you* than to a shark," I tell her. She
flashes me a big smile. "Is it? Oh, that's nice," and
gives Nick another long stroke along his side as he
comes past.

How different is this experience for these
children than if they petted wild kangaroos, for
instance, that have become tame and come in for a
hand-out of food and a bit of stroking? I did that at
one park in Victoria, where the kangaroos are not
penned at all, but are accustomed to come to a
particular place near the car-park where people
regularly feed them grain sold at the kiosk, and the
animals allow themselves to be touched
sometimes. It is very pleasing to have any wild
thing, or should we say "free" thing, voluntarily
come and let us touch it. Is it because we have done
such terrible things to so many animals that they
are all afraid of us, and so on the rare occasion that
they are not, we feel a great relief from our guilt?

Each time the dolphins give a big swish to get
themselves mobile again in the shallow water, the
children startle and jump out of the way. Only the
ones such as Kim who have spent more time with
them have ceased to be startled. Often a child who
is reaching down and petting the top of a dolphin's
beak will jerk his hand away if the dolphin opens its
mouth. Over and over I assure them, "The dolphin
won't bite you. He's just doing that because often
people have fish to give him." And parents keep
saying to the children, "Go on, it won't hurt you.
Get closer, I want to get your picture with the
dolphin!" But the children are wary. And most of
the parents do not even wade into the water at all.
Though some do, and are as delighted as the
youngsters to be allowed to touch. Why is it
humans are so often afraid of animals? I don't

believe we have nearly so often been hurt by
animals as we have hurt *them.*

3:00. A gorgeous hot summery day with a cool
breeze. (Actually August is late winter in Australia,
of course, but we are at a sub-tropical latitude.)
Only Nick and Puck are inshore, still engaging with
whoever wades into the water. People are cleaning
fish at the several crude wooden tables for that
purpose set at intervals along the beach. Others
lounge in front of their tents or caravans, enjoying a
cool beer or a cup of tea. A few boats come and go,
and several fishing boats can be seen far out over the
sand bar. The tide is fairly high and even the dog,
Ringer is out drying in the sun.

Some kids are playing with a little kayak, a few
people are swimming. The occasional dolphins
who surface now and then out in the deep, as well as
those inshore, ignore the kayak and the swimmers.
It seems odd that only people *standing* in the water
can ever touch the dolphins. Hazel told me that she
and Wilf have tried, during the slack season when
there was not another human in sight, and after
petting the dolphins for a time, to then put on face
masks and get into the water. Immediately the
dolphins leave! They just won't have anything to do
with a human immersed in the water, most
especially with one wearing a diving mask. I wanted
to get a look at Nick and Puck under the water to
see if they are males (we always call them "he"), but
I guess I'll never get that close under water.

Today a little boy named Chris who's been here
for two weeks and loves the dolphins tells me he got
to touch little Joy this morning. "I'd been feeding
fish to Puck, and Joy came right up to me and I
patted her beak," he tells me with pride and delight.
"Really?" I say. "How wonderful. She doesn't
usually come in that close, does she?" "No, she
doesn't usually." And then, you know what

happened?" He holds up a finger with two places
where the skin is barely broken. "Holey-fin came and
bit me." "My goodness!" "Yeah, I guess she didn't
want me to touch her baby." "I guess not." "She'd been
swimming around farther out, but then when I was
petting little Joy, she just came right in and bit me."
"What did you do then? Were you scared?" "Oh, I
jumped back. But I wasn't really scared, not of
Holey-fin!" He looks at me to corroborate the
absurdity of anyone being afraid of Holey-fin, that
gentle creature. "It was only," he goes on, "that she
didn't want me to touch her baby." "Yes, I'm sure
that's true." "Well, anyway," looking at his finger, "it
doesn't hurt, and I'm glad Joy came to me, even if I
don't get to pet her anymore." "Yes, that's a real honor.
Well, I guess maybe Holey-fin doesn't want Joy to
have anything to eat except what *she* gives her. And
the only way she can be sure of that is to keep her
away from our hands." "Yeah, that's probably right."

Dear little Joy. What a charmer. She swims just
beyond the others when they come to us, turning or
rolling and diving, a little bundle of sleek sweet
grace.

Puck and Nick and Holey-fin are making lots of
squealy sounds today. Some of the children are
whistling to call them, and maybe that is the reason
they respond that way. I am not a good whistler, so I
"talk" to the dolphins by making "chk" sounds,
such as one makes to a horse, with tongue, cheek
and back teeth on one side. Or I make drawn out
kissing noises with my lips, which sound much the
same as one of the kinds of sounds the dolphins
make.

One man is doing this quite loudly and very
long drawn out, and the dolphins seem interested.
His mate (Australian slang for friend) says to him, "I
hope you aren't saying something obscene in

dolphinese!"

"Aw", he says, taken aback. "Well, wouldn't an obscenity have to have *intent*? I don't mean anything obscene," he laughs. Interesting concept. He leans over a dolphin that is passing his knees just under water and makes his drawn out kissing sound again, but now he is self-conscious and stops with a laugh. "I didn't mean anything, fellas," he says to the dolphins, with a wide wave of his arm.

They are feeling very playful today, and after about each half-hour of contact with people, they tend to glide out deeper and engage in some rough and tumble among themselves. Too bad they will not tolerate us joining them. But the water is a bit too cool to be inviting. And they move all over the place so fast that a human swimmer would be left floundering in one spot, no matter how marvellously skilled he might be.

It is glorious to watch them frolic together. They often race along two or three or even four together so close that they are actually touching one another. And as they get out into deeper water, two or three together, one will often roll over lengthwise on top of the others, turning white belly up, out of the water, with its little flippers up in the

air and its back on the other dolphin. Then it rolls
on over into the water on the other side. I take
pictures of this, and surely hope they come out, but
it all happens so fast that even at 500ths of a second,
I cannot be very sure.

Sometimes there is a great splashing, with
heads and tails in all directions. Often they leap out
of the water and dive deep. Sometimes they race
very fast, just under the surface of the water with
dorsal fin showing and the flukes undulating fast as
the dolphin tears along. When they are just lazing
along, they often swim two side by side, or one just
to the side and slightly behind the other, and then
they usually will break the surface simultaneously,
slowly arching back down to disappear under water
again. It occurred to me that of course what they are
doing is taking a breath. And do you realize what
this means, that they do this so often *together*? It
means that they are swimming along breathing in
unison. Have you ever tried breathing with
someone? It is a lovely harmony. I don't mean big
loud deep conscious breaths together, but just
breathing normally with someone, so that over a
period of time, both of you alter your natural
breathing just barely enough that you are breathing
together in unison. It is a beautiful serenely
harmonic way to experience oneness. And I think
this kind of harmony and oneness is something the
dolphin experience is all about.

Thursday 28 August 80

7:00. Sun is up. One boat comes in with its net,
and four dolphin fins are visible. They turn out to be
Holey-fin, Nick, Joy, and Puck. I take a picture of
them by the boat in the long rays of the rising sun
and another of Nick eyeing me with another
dolphin close by. Two more boats come in at the
other end of the reserved beach, and the dolphins

glide over to investigate as I go for breakfast in my caravan.

At 9:00 (low tide, just starting in) a small group of children are in the water near the jetty, trying to entice Nick, the only dolphin in sight, to come to take a fish, while their parents wait with cameras up on the jetty. Nick is busy supervising the launching of a large twin-engine catamaran, a matter that requires his attention for some time. He busily swims from one side to the other, eye out of the water, as the four-wheel-drive vehicle backs the trailer carefully down the ramp. The men fumble with the catches, then rock the boat out of its cradle, and suffer delays starting the motor. Finally satisfied that the boat is going to be all right, Nick comes for his fish and allows himself to be petted and stroked. He is not really hungry, and when the first fish offered is a mangled thing, he takes it and carries it around sideways in his mouth for quite some time, just playing with it . . . dropping it in the water, turning around to pick it up, tearing off with it in a big circle and back again and finally letting it drift, eyeing it balefully. I take a picture of this last view. I suggest to the children that they pet him without feeding him, and gradually Nick lets them touch him more and more, until he is gliding very slowly past to let them give him long strokes along his side. One girl persists in trying to touch his blow-hole, and each time he gives a big puff, jerks his head and swims away fast. The amazing thing is that he still comes back! So patient and forgiving. A boy was doing that yesterday. I tried to explain to them both that he doesn't like that.

"Suppose a stranger came up to you and put fingers in your nostrils!" I have fantasies of *doing* this to the next kid I see persisting in poking the blow-hole, but I'd probably have an irate Aussie father taking a poke at *me.* It is a revelation to see how insensitive humans are with these gentle creatures. I've seen a man hold a cigarette out to the dolphin's open mouth. Many offer bread, and once there were eight slices of bread floating around in the water where people were standing and dolphins coming and going. The dolphins don't take bread, but people throw it in the water anyway.

11:30. Very flat sea and bright sun, tide rising. A number of boats are out fishing. Occasional dolphins are seen lazily surfacing at different distances out. Only Holey-fin is cruising back and forth at the shore, without even little Joy, who must be playing with the big boys farther out. When a woman brings a big packet of frozen fish down to the water's edge and starts to thaw them, breaking fish apart from one another in the water, Holey eagerly pokes her beak in among them. The woman moves into the shallowest water. "No wait, silly, they have to thaw." Holey-fin practically beaches herself in her efforts to reach the fish, but the woman is adamant that she will not give them until they are thawed. (Thank goodness. Some people *do* give frozen fish. Brrr. Poor tummy.)

Making U turns in the very shallow water, Holey-fin often shows her belly, which has brown speckles on it. None of the other dolphins who come here now have this coloration, but the dolphin who was the most tame of all when the Masons first came here almost five years ago was called Old Speckledy-belly because she had these same sorts of brown freckles on her underside. They judged her to be old because she had very few teeth left, and her mouth was drawn in as an old person's mouth usually is when the teeth are gone. Hazel wonders if speckles may be a sign of old age, and maybe Holey-fin is getting old — though, of course, she has this new baby. I wonder if perhaps Holey-fin is Old Speckledy-belly's daughter, and the markings are hereditary. But neither Nick nor Joy have them, Holey's two known off-spring.

Someone else comes with a bag of cut-up shark meat, and Nick takes a number of pieces before he finally starts to drop it in the water after taking it from the hand. Holey doesn't like it, but is still eager for the good bony herring that are being thawed. The dog Ringer is standing there chest deep getting blissed out on dolphin vibes as usual. A crowd is gathering, and still only Holey-fin and Nick are there. Three different groups of fish-offerers are giving them all to just these two dolphins.

A couple with English accents who are wreck divers are enjoying watching and photographing. They are especially fascinated with the dog-and-dolphin relationship. They tell me about a fir place to snorkle called Coral Bay up north of Carnarvon. The bay is a national preserve where

one can easily swim from the beach to snorkle over
the lovely coral and fishes. I ask them if they ever
saw any dolphins there, and they say they had, but
only from some distance. "We've not ever seen
anything to equal this anywhere. Nor heard of it
either. Look at these marvelous friendly animals.
What a lovely experience."

All this time Nick has not let me touch him
today. But finally after he's had quite a few fish, he
comes for a stroke. I ask the man to take my
photograph with him, but I don't know if the snap
happened at a really good moment. It is very
difficult to get good pictures because the movement
is always so fast.

Suddenly more dolphins are in! Puck,
Crooked-fin, and the one I think may be Beautiful's

Baby. I go up to the shop to ask for help in identifying, and Wilf comes down to the water to see.

"Yes," he say, "that's the one." He is certain because of a tiny indentation in the back of the fin about two-thirds down from the top. We agree to name it "B.B.," because it is too much of a mouthful to say Beautiful's Baby, and he is anything but a "baby" any more, a big strapping fellow.

"This one is the same age as Nick, isn't it?" I ask. "Yes, they were both tiny new-borns when we came here the summer of '76. They would have been born, we think, in December '75 or January '76." I still get confused and have to do a double take on "winter" and "summer" in Australia. "Oh yes, of course, January is summer." Wilf gives me a tolerant grin.

Nick, Puck and B.B., the three adolescents, are shouldering one another in rough play in the shallow water at our knees. B.B. is noticeably the largest, and although Nick is quite a bit larger than last year, Puck is *much* larger than last year. (It was actually a year and four months ago that I saw them before, when B.B. and Nick were just over three years old, and Puck only two, definitely a "baby" still.) In fact, Nick, age four-and-a-half, and Puck, age three-and-a-half, are just the same size now, and B.B., the same *age* as Nick, is larger. At four-and-a-half, he seems the size of the mothers (Holey-fin and Crooked-fin). Are the males of this species larger than the females? If so, might B.B. be a male, and Puck a male, and Nick a female? (Should we be calling "her" Nicki?) That might account for the discrepancy in size.

All of these dolphins seem small for *Tursiops*, the genus of dolphins commonly called bottlenosed dolphins which we see at dolphin shows and in films. The sea-circus dolphins look larger than

these animals. Holey-fin is the mother of a
four-and-a-half year old, so she must surely be fully
grown, but she cannot be more than
two-and-one-half meters long. Similarly,
Crooked-fin, whose known off-spring is
three-and-a-half years old, must also be mature, but
is only a fraction larger, if at all, than Holey-fin. By
now there are seven dolphins jostling one another
in the shallow water, and three more only five
meters offshore. None can possibly be as much as
three meters long. Are they a small species? I read
somewhere that there are "deepwater" Tursiops and
"coastal" Tursiops. Are these the coastal, and is the
coastal a smaller sub-species? Or are females
always this much smaller, and are all these
dolphins females and young? I wish there were
some expert to ask.

One older lady here, whom I've seen a number
of times, tells me that she stays here every year
while her husband fishes, and has a special rapport
with the young dolphin I call Puck. Her name for
him is "Walker," because she often takes long walks
down the beach, and he accompanies her. "He
follows right along in the water beside me as I
walk," she tells me. "I am much slower than he, so
he circles round and round, but stays right near me
all the way along. So, since he walks with me, I call
him Walker. Hello, Walker." She doesn't wade into
the water, but watches him from the sand, and he
glides past several times, tilted to one side so that
his eye is out of the water, looking at her. What a
nice relationship.

I keep thinking I'll leave and get out of the
blistering sun (my nose is like Rudolph the
reindeer), and out of my cold wet pants, but more
dolphins keep coming, and I'm too fascinated to
tear myself away.

Beautiful, with her feather shaped scar, is here,

and out from shore the one with a ragged fin that I dubbed Rags is passing back and forth.

Now Nick is in the mood to be stroked and petted. He (or she?) repeatedly comes up to me, beak close to my knees and just under the water, with only the blowhole above the surface. I stroke the top of the beak, and also under the "chin." Sometimes the mouth is slightly open, just at water level, and I rub all around on the hard rubbery beak.

After a few rubs on the beak, "Nicki" will turn and glide slowly past me as I press my palm against her side. (Today I seem to feel quite sure our old friend Nick is a female.) The harder I press, the harder she presses in toward me. Puck comes too, and gets a good beak scratch. He seems to prefer an *under-the-chin* rub, and the skin is very hard and rough there, as if it is scar tissue. They do seem to collect many wounds — a rough life, somehow. He is a little more shy about a stroke along the side, although he obviously likes it. I'm likely to have to lean far over to reach him as he glides by. This leaves a space between him and my knees, and several times Nick crowds in between, and shoves Puck away, and they go off jostling one another. Then B.B. comes in for a good chin rub and likes to be stroked all over the head. He seems especially — well, *happy* somehow, every time I see him. This is the dolphin about whom several people have especially felt, "That dolphin is trying to tell me something." He looks right into your eye with that marvelous joyful look that is such a direct personal contact.

It is interesting that people think, "I wonder what the message is?" Do we wonder that because we are expecting some words? Or some directive? — "Go and do so-and-so." Anyway, it is just wonderful to be standing here in the water with them, stroking them, looking into their eyes, hearing their little sounds. It is a sort of rapidly-stuttering soft squeal. The nearest sound I can make is a long kissing sound, which seems to delight them.

Nicki is coming in again and again for long strokes. When she crowds against my knees, over and over, I can stroke her far side as she presses her near side against me and slides past. Others are also crowding around — Puck and Holey-fin, Crooked-fin, B.B., Little Joy and some others just beyond. Always movement, movement.

At one pass, just as I am starting to give her a stroke, Nicki turns right over on her back, belly up, little flippers up in the air, and glides swiftly by, then twists over again and pushes into a crowd of other dolphins. What a surprise! Before I knew what

was happening, I was stroking her white belly. Often I've seen them roll over that way in play together, but not with people.

Holey-fin is suckling baby Joy now, and they glide past, only a meter away. They weave in and out among the other dolphins, coming in closer than I've ever seen Joy before. So the incident of the boy touching Joy the other day has not scared Holey-fin away from letting the baby come in close. What a dear sweet little thing it is. It leaps in the air much more often than the larger ones, but I have not been able yet to catch that on film.

Who are the others out there? There is that one with a long narrow verticle slice out of the back edge of the fin that was here the other day. And one with a big dark smooth fin with no marks. I don't know who that is — it is not coming in close. Much rough and tumble.

Today I try the "Sea Voice" gadget that Wade
Doak gave me when I visited him in New Zealand.
It is a mouthpiece fitted with a rubber balloon to
immerse in the water and speak into, so that the
sound is conducted underwater. During a time that
only Holey-fin is in, and the others are cavorting
farther out, I try several times to call them in.
"Nick, here Nick, chk, chk, chk," clucking my
tongue against the back teeth and making kissing
sounds. None of the dolphins seem to pay any
attention. Later, when they are in close, I try it
again, and Nicki comes over and noses the balloon
in the water once, but I couldn't say that she really
responded.

Once today some children playing with a large
rubber ball lost it in the water, and it went floating
out. The multi-colored ball, floating gently out on
the cool blue-green sea, was a pretty sight. Dolphins
were playing all around, but paid no attention at all.
Finally a father was summoned to swim out and
retrieve it. The dolphins clearly have no interest at
all in "foreign objects." Fish are the only objects I
have ever seen them "play" with. And of course
each other.

Well, what a day! How many have come now?
Holey-fin, Joy, Nick, Puck, B.B., and Crooked-fin
are all close in. Out deeper the two unnamed ones
plus the one I called Notch the other day. The two
unnamed dolphins swim exactly side by side like
twins, breathing together, with Notch often as a
close third member of the team. Lovely. Much
farther out, an occasional dark grey body arches out
of the water for a breath and dives again.

It is 2:30. I have not eaten lunch. I'm cold and
hungry and sunburned. I must go and wash my hair
and get ready to go into town to teach a yoga class
and visit with new friends. But what a day! What a
glorious day!

I had dinner and spent much of the evening with Jan and Barry who own the Post Office store in Denham, the town of some 300 inhabitants which is a half-hour drive from the caravan park. Also present were Lee Ann, who works in the store during this rush tourist season, and Laurie, a fisherman. Jan and Barry spent some time a couple of years ago doing a study of sharks in Shark Bay. There are more sharks, and a larger variety of sharks, here than anywhere else they know of in the world, with some species not even identified. While it is true that there are a large number of shark incidents in Australia, relative to the small population of this country, they point out that: (1) Australia has enormous mileage of beach front, (2) nearly *all* Aussies swim in the sea — a very high incidence of sea swimming per population which increases the exposure to the possibility of shark contact, and (3) the reporting of shark "incidents" includes even the sighting of a shark, often reported as a shark "chasing me", which may be very subjective. Aussies train their children from birth to "watch out" for snakes and sharks, and that does instill fear. Of course it is true that when a shark does bite, it is a terrible wound, often involves the loss of a limb, or at least a hand or foot, or a great chunk of arm or thigh muscle, so that there is irreparable maiming. Barry said, "The shark is capable of tearing our greater mouthfuls than any other marine creature, and is a voracious eater." But these incidents are really few in number, they say, it is just that they are so horrible when they occur, and so played up in the news. A shark incident is reported prominently in newspapers all over the world, while the story of a youth horribly maimed in a motorcycle accident is so commonplace that it is found only in the back pages of the local paper.

We discuss a bit about how humans love to

scare ourselves, watching scary movies, children
telling each other ghost stories. Fear is really a
sought-after sensation. "How about here in Shark
Bay? Are there many incidents here, where there
are so many sharks? Have people been attacked
often?"

"No, none"

"None at all?"

"None. Only one undocumented story from
100 years ago that a man lost his hand. These sharks
are so well fed — these waters are so teeming with
food. And sharks don't really want to eat people.
They normally go for much smaller fish. Probably
we aren't that palatable to them," says Barry.

We talked about what it is like to live in
Denham year round, a little village of perhaps 300
population that is a full three hour drive from a
town of larger size, and even that is only about
20,000.

"It's quite nice, actually. A very quiet, simple,
wholesome life, great for the kids. We have good
friends. We enjoy each other, and probably family
life looms larger for us than for city people. We like
our house (it *is* handsome and comfortable) and it
has all the 'mod cons' (Aussie slang for 'modern
conveniences'). We enjoy having the store and post
office, with the people-contact it brings. It's only for
three weeks twice a year, at the May and August
school holidays, that it's so madly busy, as it is now.
Most of the time it's very easy."

"What about the longer summer holidays at
Christmas time?" (this time I'd got my seasons
straight) "Don't you get a flock of visitors then?"

"No, we don't. It's very hot in this part of
Australia then, you know, and people think it
would be just too hot. At that time of year, the Perth
people go south for their holidays where it's cooler.
But we don't find it bad here at all in the summer.

That's when we get our wind, especially on this side of the peninsula. Right here on the water, the breeze is always pleasant in summer. And we all love the sea so much, and have the kind of life that gives us time to enjoy it." Sounds very nice.

"Do you have dolphin friends here as they do over at Monkey Mia?"

"Oh, there are dolphins around here, all right from time to time. Everywhere you go in Shark Bay you might run into dolphins, but not the friendly ones that let you pet them, as those do. That's unique, I believe."

"Do you suppose they ever swim around to this side of the peninsula?"

"Well, it's a long way. Must be 40 kilometers north of here to the tip of the peninsula, and Monkey Mia is about 50 kilometers back down the other side; so that would be 90 kilometers around (over 50 miles). No reason why they *couldn't* do it, I'm sure, but we don't know that anyone ever saw Nick or Holey-fin over here. They seem quite happy where they are." True enough.

Friday 29 August 80

7:00. Sun is up, low tide, calm and clear. Nick and Puck are cruising the shore. Holey-fin and Joy are helping the boats in and out. One man draws his boat in on the sand and goes up to a big tent on the beach to get his wife and small daughter to show them something in the boat. It is a fat, strangely soft-looking fish, half a meter long. He holds it up by a hook. "This is a blowie," he says to the child very seriously. "It bites very hard. It will take your toe off. So look out for it if you're in the water. Come out of the water if you see one."

The child, held in mum's arms, looks appropriately awed.

"Is that the one they also call toadfish?" I ask.

"Yes. One took a little girl's toe right off here last year."

"Here? At Monkey Mia?"

"Yes, I think so."

"Show her the teeth", the mother says. The father pries the mouth open with a beer can opener. "There, see all those teeth?" he asks sternly. Rows of flat-topped teeth, meeting together. "They'll take your toe or finger off."

Meddler me, I had to put in, "*Can* take your toe off. Not necessarily *will*."

I walk away to the dolphins, with a little sinking feeling. It is sad to see children being taught to fear the sea. Can we teach them caution without fear? What is the best way to do that?

I took some black-and-white photos, thinking it might be easier to reproduce them in black and white if I publish the notes I'm making.

2:00. The tide is high now, and the dolphins are playing out deep. I try to photograph leaps, but the leap usually is finished before I can point the camera.

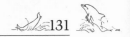

Since no dolphins are inshore, I decide to deviate from my normal pattern by feeding them fish today. So I pay Hazel fifty cents for a packet of frozen yellowtails. It takes quite a time for them to thaw. After a half-hour in the sun, I separate them and lay them out on the sand at water's edge, then take one out into the water with me and swish it around to thaw in the sea . . . and to attract dolphins. The little boy, Kim, is there, having been slapping the water with his hand, hoping for dolphins for some time. And faithful Ringer is there.

Sure enough, by the time I've swished the fish through the water three or four times, here comes a grey streak through the water, like an arrow straight toward me. "Well, hello Nicki. That didn't take you long." Puck is coming too, from another direction. Out of all the things that are going on along this shore, and out there in the sea, how is it that they know at once that someone has a fish in hand for them? They must be aware of *everything* in great detail. As I comment on this, a young man on shore says, "They must smell it." I say, "No, they have no sense of smell at all." I'd just read that in the Encyclopedia of Australian Fishing. "They have very sharp eyesight, both above and under water. And then you know they have this amazing sound-location system, like sonar or radar." "Well, it works well, doesn't it!" he laughs.

Here comes Holey-fin. They really want my fish. But it still is stiff, and I don't want to give them something that will chill the belly. Holey-fin and Puck go away when no feeding is happening, but Nick persists. I *want* to hold it in the water to thaw it, but he almost grabs it out of my hand. "No, wait, love, it has to thaw, it's too cold for you." I hold it behind my back and he swims around behind me, almost beaching himself. "You silly thing." Since he's so eager, I think it's a good chance to try to get

him to lift his head out of the water, holding the fish
above his head temptingly. But they rarely lift right
out. Usually they open their mouths just at the
surface, with the lower jaw and eyes under water.

Then I try enticing him to swim through my
legs, by standing with feet wide apart and holding
the fish behind me in the water. But he swishes
away in disgust, as if to say, "Don't play games with
me!" Did he read my mind, that I would have
snatched the still cold fish up out of reach if he had
gone for it?

He's back, though, after a few fast circles out in
deeper water. I guess it is finally limp enough, so I
put it gently into his mouth, head first. "There you
are," and give him a pat. They always swim off as
they swallow, but he's back again with mouth open
for more fish. I turn toward the fish I'd left on the
sand.

The gulls! A whole flock of the pale and elegant
little Red-legged Gulls are there pecking at my fish!
It's a wonder they haven't taken them all. But

perhaps they don't like them frozen. (I never gave gulls credit for such discretion.) All five fish are still there. It takes a long time to thaw each one in the water, and Nick and Puck keep pestering me. Puck gives up more easily, so Nick gets the second fish as well. Then I decide I'm *not* going to give them all to him! He tries to crowd Puck out when I'm determined to feed it to him. Pushy brat! But I get it into Puck's mouth. Kim wants to feed one, and that one goes to Nick. Come on, I thought. I want to see some of the other dolphins. I notice a feeling in myself that I'm not getting the show that I paid my ticket for. How interesting is the working of the mind.

I leave the last two fish on the sand with Kim to guard and try to get in some good dolphin stroking as I did yesterday. But they are really not interested and won't pass me close for a stroke at all. After a while I give up trying. Only Nick has stayed around, so I think maybe if I give him another fish, he'll come for a pet. He takes it, but lets me touch him only on the beak.

A little girl about nine or ten years old who has been thrilled over watching them, trying to get brave enough to try to touch them, asks if she can give a fish. Holey-fin has joined us again, so I give the child the last fish, saying, "Here, give it to the mother. Now don't let Nick grab it." I push Nick aside, and he splashes a big spray of water on me with his tail. Holey-fin comes up gently, and stays very still with open beak so that the child can approach and lay the fish in her mouth. As the mouth closes, the starry-eyed child pats the top of the beak, and Holey-fin gently glides away. A very satisfying encounter. The girl looks up at me in speechless glory, and as I look into her eyes we share our dolphin love. Kim is watching us with a little half-smile of satisfaction and understanding, as if to say, "Welcome to the club." He and Ringer have been raptly watching, participating by just being there.

An hour later I come down to find this little girl feeding another packet of fish to a mob of dolphins, with parents on shore taking photographs. There are Holey-fin, Nick, Puck, Crooked-fin and Beautiful, with little Joy dashing in and out among them, and a couple of others off shore. There is that one with the narrow slice out of the back edge of the fin, and I can't get a good look at the other, but it may be B.B. Those two are gliding back and forth closely side by side.

Still none of them will let me stroke them. I try to get a photo of Holey-fin and Joy suckling, but it is too hard to get an angle where I can see the baby clearly. And they go by so fast, it is almost impossible to adjust the distance for good focus. I've used up the roll of black-and-white and hope I have some good ones, since there is not another roll of black-and-white in all of Denham (three stores!). I still have a last roll of Ektachrome.

The young girl is petting each dolphin as it comes to her, mostly a firm touch on top of the beak with her soft little hand, but occasionally a short stroke on the back behind the blowhole. Often they are skittish about being touched there, as both the blowhole and the dorsal fin seem to be places that they feel insecure about being touched. But they are trusting her completely. They are being very gentle with her, although also excited and frisky as one by one they circle away between encounters. She is in a state of quiet ecstasy, very poised and confident with them, and very happy. It is lovely to see.

I went back to my caravan and reflected on my feelings. I recognize a strong desire to have something *happen* in the relationship with the dolphins. I realize that we humans tend to want a

relationship to develop, especially if it has much warmth in it. We want new ways of demonstrating and being demonstrated to. We want some drama in an emotional relationship. It is hard to be content with having things just go along uneventfully. I also noted that I felt disappointed that Nick had not let me cuddle him as he had yesterday. It was the old phenomenon of expectation — attachment to what we want to happen. "Attachment is the cause of all suffering," as the Buddha said. I observe in myself the feelings of a rejected lover.

Another thing I realize, looking back, is that my behavior today was not typical of me. I did not make any of my usual sounds. Why was that? I just forgot to make my kissing and chucking noises. And I fed them fish. I acted like the other tourists. And I got treated like one.

To compensate myself, I indulged in a large meal. I made potato salad just the way I like it, cooking the onions with the potatoes, then adding chopped celery and sweet pickles and hard-boiled egg, with lots of mayonnaise. I made enough to last for two days, but after eating half, it tasted so good that I kept eating more and more. I'd also had plenty of vegetables and cheese, and my stomach was quite satisfactorily full, but my mouth was still enjoying the taste sensations, and I ate all of the potato salad! Then an hour later I went over to the shop and had a raspberry-ripple double ice cream cone. I walked along the beach in the dark licking the delicious ice cream, and pondering the phenomenon of gluttony.

But only at an intellectual level. My stomach was complaining somewhat by this time, but my mouth was still rejoicing in all the indulgence.

Do dolphins ever do this, overeat to this degree? (Are they out there watching me?) Do any wild animals ever do it, eat more than is even healthy? It is my impression that they don't, though of course domestic animals do. Especially dogs, of all animals probably the most influenced by humans. Poor dears.

I remember reading some statistics that overweight is the most widespread cause of ill health in America, and that more money is spent on diet pills and commercial programs that promise to help you lose weight, in Europe and America, than on those countries' aid programs to populations that are undernourished. If everyone on this earth ate as we do, we would soon strip the planet of all its nourishment. Why do we do it, even to the point of intestinal discomfort?

I walked along the beach, pondering these grave thoughts. And licking my luscious raspberry ripple ice cream, delighting in the sweetly tangy fruit flavor and the delectable creamy richness of it all. Yum yum! Marvelous indulgence in taste sensation.

Saturday 30 August 80

7:00.The sun is just rising, a giant flaming ball sandwiched between the horizon and a heavy grey cloud. Dolphins are silhouetted against the fiery light reflected in the water. (And this once I didn't bring my camera!) Holey-fin and her two children, Nick and Joy, are there, and Puck appears soon. People in fishing camps are early risers, and there is much activity of boats and nets and breakfast calls for children. Several youngsters are already standing in the water to pet the dolphins and to hand out a few fish from nets already brought in. But pickings seem slim — not very many fish in the nets this morning.

There is a pleasant family I haven't seen before. The parents are waiting to go for a beach walk, but the children are sidetracked by dolphins.

"Aren't they lovely," the mother murmurs,

smiling. "We were down here sitting on the end of the jetty to all hours last night, and they were there in the moonlight, quietly swimming around. After the generator went off at eleven, it was so nice to have this beautiful silence, and now and then hear the dolphins blow." She glances at me hesitantly to see if I am with her in this sentiment.

"It's a wonderful sound, isn't it," I encourage her.

"Yes, marvelous. It seemed to express in sound all the other sensory details — the bay, the moonlight, the vast space, the life in the sea . . . " We stand side by side in companionable reflection, gazing out across the water. I have never seen the dolphins at night, but from her eloquent little description I have a very real experience of being there that night.

"What a beautiful place it is here," she says. "I love the desert."

"It's unusual for me to have the desert next to the sea," I tell her. "All the other beach places I've ever been have had trees near by — at least palm trees."

"That's a nice sort of beach, too," she says. "But here there are these desert wattles and all these wildflowers, little herbaceas things pushing through the sand. And those big red cliffs with caves, and the dunes. It's all beautiful in such a quiet subtle way. And then these gorgeous friendly creatures. What a treat!"

We watch the dolphins for a half-hour before the family finally sets off on their beach exploration, and I go to breakfast.

Then I take a three-hour-long beach walk myself, off around the point to the right (east and then south), exploring the sand bars at low tide with Pluto, the Mason's black Labrador dog for company. I enjoy the gulls and terns, and watch two big

black-and-white pelicans sailing majestically. A
whole colony of cormorants stand on a sand bar
until Pluto gallops into their midst and scatters
them. There are big red-billed Caspian terns, little
godwits, and tiny sandpipers.

The water is very shallow around here, and at
low tide one can walk far, far out, only barely
wetting the feet. Shell collectors like to come here
to find beautiful specimens. One of the favorites is
the Bailer shell, named for its use in bailing the
water from small boats. The large smooth
ballonlike lip is very handsome, and nowadays the
shell is often used to make lamps. I have admired
these lamps and thought that I would like to have
one to provide a soft light in a room, but have
hesitated to buy one because I do not like to
encourage the destruction of shell life for

commercial purposes. What I would like to happen
is that I would find a handsome specimen already
dead, but recently enough that the shell is still
smooth and shiny. While I was staying at the Great
Barrier Reef last month, some of my acquaintances
were in the business of collecting shells for sale, and
would come home with a whole bucketful of live
specimens of some particular fine species and boil
them up. I did not feel good about this. It seemed
greedy. I had a hard time with my feelings toward
those people, although *they* felt that they had a very
nice way of making a living, in touch with nature
all the time.

Anyway, here I am, having a lovely day
paddling along in the shallow water, picking up
pretty little cockle shells and watching the birds.
Tide still going out, so that I wander farther and
farther from shore. On the sand bar just appearing
above water ahead of me I see a big lump under the
sand. Going to investigate, I find it is a fist sized
volute, a shellfish whose shell is a beautiful granite
grey, mottled light and dark. As the tide goes out,
these snail-like creatures push up from under the
sand and glide out into the shallow water to feed.
The mantle spreading out from the aperture is
mottled grey like the shell, and has a vivid yellow
edge. Beautiful. All the marvelous designs of
nature! There are several more on this one sandbar.
I select an especially handsome one to take back to
the camp to photograph. Then at my caravan I save
it in a tin of sea water until I get around to taking it
back to where I had found it, an hour's walk away.

At 2:00 in the afternoon I go back to see what
our dolphin friends are up to. The tide is coming in,
fairly calm, hot sun. Some adults are in the water
this time, and two adolescent boys. Fish are being
thawed on the sand by a woman sitting in her swim
togs in the edge of the water. Old regulars,

Holey-fin, Nick and Puck, are crowding in. There is
one more. Let's see . . . it is B.B. They jostle one
another and lift open beaks toward outstretched
hands, accept a tentative pat from a half-frightened
hand, then swirl away to glide off parallel to the
beach. They take a turn out into the deeper water,
then glide by again, eye out of the water to see if any
more is happening with the fish. It is beautiful to
watch the great smooth powerful bodies.

As they glide past in depth that allows only
inches above and below, they seem not to be
moving a muscle. But if they get frisky and take off
fast, the tail sweeps up and down, the whole body
undulates powerfully, and the water makes deep
waves as they go tearing past. There is hardly any
splash, I've noticed, even when they leap out of the
deep water. Only when they wrestle with one
another do they splash a bit. Or if some human tries
to touch them unwanted, especially the blowhole
area, they may give a big swish of the tail that
splashes. Sometimes they even seem to do this on
purpose, as in fact just now, when someone crowds
in between two dolphins trying to stroke their
backs while the dolphins are reaching for fish. The
hand touches a blowhole, and WHAP! A great
shower of spray drenches us all as the indignant
dolphin (Holey-fin) thrashes her way clear of Puck,
Nick and B.B. to dash off to sea, Puck and B.B.
folowing.

Here I am dripping and laughing, but the
frightened kids have rushed off to shore. I am
concerned about my camera which has drops of
water on it, but not for the first time. I hope it
survives this two week stint.

Standing deep in the water, I turn facing the
beach to share this experience with the people, and
someone says, "Oh, look out, it's behind you!" I turn
to find Nick's head at my hip, and give his side a

stroke. "Hello, Nicki, love." There is nothing to be alarmed about. Again here is that underlying fear that humans have so often. It's really marvelous to be able to stand among these jostling big muscular bodies and feel their power and grace.

Beautiful joins the others in play four meters out. She and B.B. swim together for a long time, mother and son, sides touching. While the others stay out for a while, Nick gets all the fish! Not much will distract him when a good tasty fish is around.

When B.B. comes to join in the group play, Nick seems to take a role somewhat different from his

usual one. I have never seen Nick shove B.B. aside as
he often does with Puck, for example. The games
among the three of them are equally vigorous, or
even more so, but there is a fine quality of
coordination and harmony when B.B. is there. The
rowdiness is absent, even though there may be
much intensity. In fact there is more of a feeling
that Nick may be a female, with older and younger
male cousins she has grown up with, playing
familiar games that are beginning to have a
different meaning now she is maturing. Nick is
often the star of the act, even with B.B. there. In the
game I call "dolphin roll-over", when three swim
fast abreast and then the middle one rolls over
lengthwise upside down on the back of one of the
others, Nick is usually the middle one who does the
roll-over.

The mother dolphins, Holey-fin, Crooked-fin
and Beautiful, also join in all the games, and are as
vigorous and playful as the youngsters. Other
participants are Notch, Rags and Sickle-fin (males
or females?) whenever they are visiting the beach.
And of course baby Joy is much involved. Dolphins
of all ages seem to love to nudge and rub against her,
to stroke her with their flippers, and to chase and
tumble with her. Any one may also stay beside her
very calmly sometimes, just drifting, with very
little movement. It is very rare that any of these
dolphins stays still in one spot — they are
constantly on the move, and the few times I have
noticed one just drifting quietly in the water, little
Joy has been beside that one, whether it be
Holey-fin, Crooked-fin, Puck, B.B. or Nick.

Nick is making up for yesterday by being very
attentive today. He comes past very languidly, and
rubs his beak all around in the cup of my hand. I
stroke him first on one side and then the other, then
along the back, then on both sides at once, using

both hands. Then he comes up to me and I stretch out my hand to rub his beak, he gently takes my fingers in his mouth. I feel the sharp little teeth, but they only caress, not bite. Once he takes my wrist in his mouth in this way.

Dolphins are very tactile, love to rub against one another, and will do that with me too, now that they've come to know me well. But only if I am standing. How I wish they would let me swim with them, close that way. Maybe if I could stay longer. Maybe next year . . . .

After this they become very frisky and playful. Many grey bodies are racing and tumbling through the water and dashing among the forest of legs and

out again, rolling over one another as they drift
farther out into the deep. There is a particular game
they play that looks such fun: when two are
swimming side by side, one will lift its head up over
the back of the other and then slide its whole body
over to the other side of the first one. A sort of
sideways leapfrog. I think I managed to get a good
snapshot of this.

Another interesting maneuver is the way they
come to a stop in front of one of us. Generally they
glide back and forth in the water parallel to the
beach, and when they approach us, it is from the
side as they are diverted from this parallel glide.
They move quite swiftly, even when they are
making very little effort, so that there is quite a

strong momentum as they approach, and they manage to stop abruptly in front of us by turning the body suddenly at a right angle and quickly humping up in the middle. This movement seems to act as a brake, and they come to a dead stop (momentarily). Their agility is most admirable, as well as their apparently absolute awareness of where they are at any given time relative to each other and us and the ocean floor. The pause in front of us is usually very brief indeed, but I try to photograph Puck in the hump position. In seconds they give a big swish of the powerful body and are away again. The scene is one of constant movement. Even when we are petting them, it is usually as they glide past. Only for a good snout rub will they hold still for a few seconds, or to get a fish into the mouth.

There are many visitors coming and going today, at the height of the school holiday season, and the dolphins are in a high energy mood, seemingly stimulated by all the attention. Nine or ten dolphins can be counted at any one time all afternoon, some among the crowd of people standing in the shallows, and some drifting or playing out deeper. Right up until nearly sunset they are there, and then the numbers begin to thin. As the light begins to fade, no dolphins are in sight.

The family of the little boy Kim, who has been such a devoted dolphin watcher, are leaving in the morning, and I remind him to write something for me about the dolphins. So he comes to me a little later with a piece of paper, shyly.

"What have you there?" I ask him.

"I wrote a poem about the dolphins," he tells me.

"Wonderful. May I see it?" So he gives it to me. (Here it is, as I told him that if I published a book about the dolphins I would include his poem.)

He wrote:

DOLPHINS

Dolphins have skin so rubbery and warm.
They like to eat fish from when they are born.
They are very intelligent and are so cute.
When they speak they sound like a lovely flute.
                                    —Kim Ingle

"That's a very fine poem. Thank you very much! They do have lovely skin, don't they?" I comment.

"Yes, it's nice to touch it. It feels like wet velvet."

"You're right, you know. That is what it feels like. A very unusual texture." (Wet velvet! What a perfect description. Soft and silky, with a sort of depth of texture.)

What a good experience for a child to have had, to have spent many hours with Ringer at his side, stroking dolphins and feeling their showers of echo clicks flowing over him, day after day. I expect he will never forget.

Sunday 31 August 80

At 7:00, sun is up, sky clear, light breeze. Tide is going low. Three boats are just coming in with their nets. No dolphin in sight. I watch one couple pull in their boat and start to clean the net. Lots of seaweed, few fish.

At 10:00, tide low, a crowd of Sunday visitors are near the pier, with Holey-fin, Nick, Puck and Crooked-fin coming in for pats on the beak, to the delight of the crowd, cameras snapping. I photograph this from up on the pier, showing the colorful tents and caravans in the background. With the tide so low, the water is dense with muck from the bottom, and it is interesting to see that our dolphin friends seem to pay no attention. Although their eyesight is keen, the scientists tell us, they do not need to see with their eyes, having other ways of

detecting shapes and locations, and, I feel sure, of detecting attitudes and intentions. Several other dolphins can be seen farther out.

2:00. Crooked-fin and Puck are swimming lazily near the pier. No others in sight. (Again, it sometimes looks as if he is suckling. Is it possible after three-and-a-half?) Some children are playing with a big inner tube, and others are swimming nearby. The two dolphins keep well away from the swimmers.

The camp is very full of people and very busy. Vehicles coming and going, boats being launched, or being pulled out of the water, tents being set up or taken down, laundry flapping on the clotheslines, children and dogs and elderly people mixed among the fishermen. The smell of cooking fish is constant in the air all week, except just at the first grey light of dawn! Hazel and Wilf are constantly in demand for the thousand little matters that need attention, to hook up a new caravan to the water and electricity, to see about the hot water, to mend this and provide that. There is a steady stream of youngsters in and out of the tiny shop, buying "lollies" (Aussie slang for candy, cookies, ice cream, and sweets of all kinds). And of course their elders need the frozen meat, fresh and tinned fruit and vegetables, soap, torch batteries ("flashlight" to us), fishing line, sun hats, today's delivery of bread, cakes and newspapers. Young Noel Mason, who lives and works in Denham, comes out to help a little on his time off, and daughter Jenny and her husband from Perth are here for a few days also. But Hazel is steadily busy in the shop for hour after hectic hour. It is a very different scene for these two weeks than the quiet camp I visited last year, when it was in its more usual state.

On this particular day, I find that it is a bit too much for me, and I am grateful for my caravan

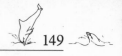
where I can be alone in the quiet to read. When I left
the beach at noon there had been a mob scene going
on there. Nick, Puck, Holey-fin, Crooked-fin, B.B.,
and Beautiful were all coasting in and out among a
sea of legs, with Joy and a few other big dolphins
cavorting in deeper water. Fish in all stages of frost
or freshness or decomposition were being offered,
as well as bits of paper or apple or whatever anyone
happened to have in hand. All in a pleasant enough
spirit, but I was feeling crowded. The dolphins,
though, must be enjoying it, or they would go away!
Today I feel particularly grateful for the fact that
these dolphins are free. They can turn right around
and leave any time it gets too heavy for them.

They are not permitting any petting today,
however. They move excitedly in and out among
the people, snatching at fish, then dropping them as
they swim away, swishing away irritably whenever
someone tries to stroke them. I feel better to be in
my caravan, away from it all.

But I am somewhat dismayed over another
matter as well. The volute shell that I had brought
from the far sand bar to photograph, then had kept
in a container of water overnight, had been
forgotten. And when I finally took a look, the soft
body was hanging limply out of its shell. After I had
been quite sanctimonious about how wrong it was
to kill these creatures for their shells! Had I really,
at some unconscious level, wanted the pretty shell
to take home to America so much that I had let it
die? I boiled it up to get rid of the flesh before it
became too odorous. The shell was indeed lovely.
But I was not enjoying it very much.

Not a very good day.

In the later afternoon, after a walk off to the
west along the beach, I come back to my caravan
and settle down for a long meditation. Deep quiet
in dolphin-ness, drifting in deep quiet

under-sea-ness. Profound quiet and with-ness.
Dark and deep and quiet water-ness. Vibrant and
living wholeness. Warm and quiet and deep and
sure aliveness.

At sunset I go out on the now still beach. The
dolphins have left. Most campers are in their tents
and caravans. As I stroll the beach alone, a land
breeze brings the sweet smell of wildflowers from
across the sand dunes behind the caravans. The
little welcome swallows flit close by, squeaking
much as the dolphins squeak.

All sounds and all sights are one. All is one.

Monday 1 September 80

6:30. In the early light, no dolphins. I have
never found them here, ever, before sunrise.

6:45. There is perfectly clear sky, and brisk
breeze. A delicate rosy glow is increasing in
intensity, but still delicate. Then suddenly there is
the sun!, showing a tiny spot of pure orange light,
growing and growing to a half-round, then rising
into its full glowing disc, throwing dancing orange
sparkles across the water. the whole earth scene is
still surprisingly low lit, the cloudless sky still
delicately tinted, the orange orb itself, though fiery,
still possible to look upon.

No dolphins.

At 9:00, the tide is going low, still no dolphins.
I go with Wilf into town in the truck — his run for
mail, newspapers and bread. "The only time I get a
chance to talk with you is when you're driving," I
josh him. "That's too true! Good thing it's for only
two weeks, twice a year. I'd never stand this pace for
more than that." We comment on how well
everyone gets along in the campground, with such
limited facilities. There are only ten toilets and ten
showers, two water tanks for drinking water
(trucked from town), with brackish water from the

"bore" (artesian well) piped into the "amenity block" for showers, laundry, toilets and wash basins. I've heard very little quarrelling among the children.

But Wilf says there have been some angry feelings among the adults about bait-fish nets. They are required by order of the law to be kept 800 meters from the jetty. Then, in areas where they are permitted, they must be 50 meters apart. There are certain choice areas, and at this holiday time there are many fishermen who want to set their nets. One who leaves his "pegs" (stakes on the beach) to tie his net to the next night gets furious if someone else uses them for his own net. But Wilf says it is not legal to save a place. Another fisherman must be allowed to have it the next night if he wants it.

"Some think there shouldn't be any nets allowed any more, because many fish are destroyed. All the fish they don't want to use for bait are killed. If you get a fish on a *line* that you don't want, too small or the wrong kind, you'll usually throw it back. But in the net, they're usually destroyed. So there's agitation to get nets outlawed, and those who want nets are hot under the collar about that."

I comment on old-timers who have talked to me bemoaning the old days when fish were much more plentiful.

Wilf answers indignantly, "Yes, and they'll tell you how many fish they used to take — 300 whiting in one evening off the end of the jetty!"

"Without a net?"

"Yes, just pulling them in. And now they wonder why there aren't so many anymore. It takes fish to make more fish."

We muse about whether the dolphins would go away if the fish get much more scarce. "Well, there still seem to be quite a number of fish in this bay, compared to other places in the world. But it is certainly a possibility."

I want to talk about the experience yesterday, with so many people all wanting to touch the dolphins, and how they would not let us stroke them as they had on other days. Just too many strange people touching, touching. I comment about how it was for Hazel in the shop. All day several persons at a time all trying to get her attention. After a week of this, how exhausting it becomes. Her eyes, that usually look so attentively into those of the person she is conversing with, become unseeing, and she looks very tired and distracted. "Now imagine," I say, "if they all wanted to *touch* her too. Imagine how that would be." I pick at his shoulder several times with my fingers. "Imagine a dozen people at a time all trying to touch you, and as those leave, by twos and threes, others come. It's too much."

He drives along in silence, shaking his head, lips pressed together. "That's why we need a warden," he finally comments. "You really do need to limit it, I think. At least during these times of the year when the holiday-makers are here."

He agrees. "But then, here's the dilemma," he goes on. "When you see the experience some children have . . . you see them fall in love. Looking into the dolphin's eyes, stroking the smooth skin, then watching them go away to leap and frolic so joyfully. If visitors aren't allowed to touch them, and get in there and have that personal encounter . . . it would be a pity." Wilf glances at me as he drives.

"Yes, we don't want to have that stop," I agree. He shakes his head. "What to do? And you know, it could get to be crowded this way all year long."

"Yes, I suppose it could," I say. But I think of how far we are from the mobs of the world's people, and I don't really think it would become so crowded

any time in our lifetime. Still, it is a very difficult problem.

After a pause to ponder all this, he goes on to tell me about the day when the Japanese cameramen came, the day before the storm struck in March of 1979. A team of cameramen from a Japanese television station had come to try to film the dolphins at Monkey Mia, but had not had much luck, as not many dolphins had been around. Then the warnings came that a big windstorm was on its way to Shark Bay and due to strike that night. So Hazel and Wilf were working very hard to tie down everything movable and get as much as possible indoors. A man friend was helping, and also their daughter Sally. The cameramen were following them around taking pictures and not helping as much as might be. It was a long, hot dirty job, with no little anxiety attached.

As things began to seem about as well taken care of as possible under the circumstances, Hazel and Wilf began to speak of going into the water for a refreshing swim. Even if things weren't completely finished, Wilf thought it would be very nice to get cool and clean in the water. Sally wasn't sure for some reason that she wanted to go in, and the others were getting the idea that it might be jolly fun to dunk her. So by the time the group headed for the beach, there was considerable pushing and joking, and the camera was on the pier to capture it all on film. As the little group of frolicking humans splashed into the sea, a group of frolicking dolphins appeared also. Wilf told me that it was a wild and wonderful splashing party, with dolphins leaping and dancing and diving, and humans laughing and splashing one another. It must have made a wonderful film sequence.

"Did you ever see it?"

"No, only a black and white still print. I don't

suppose anyone would ever see the film outside of
Japan." (How I'd like to try to locate that film, I
thought. Of course it may have been erased long
since.)

That storm had done terrible damage,
including destroying the pier at Monkey Mia. Much
damage was sustained at Denham as well. Then
Wilf told me of an incident reported by some of the
people living on the Denham side.

It seems that great piles of seaweed were
washed up on the beaches all over the Peron
Peninsula, in some cases as much as a meter or
more deep on the sand. Some Denham people
walking on the beach heard sounds that seemed to
be the whistling sounds that dolphins make,
coming from a deep pile of seaweed, and they dug in
to investigate. They found a baby dolphin. Because
of the wet seaweed it had not been exposed to the
sun and drying air, and seemed to be all right, so
they helped it back into the water, and it swam
away.

Some other people, not knowing of this
incident, were on a beach somewhat farther away
from town, and also had the experience of hearing
dolphin-like whistles, and dug into the seaweed to
investigate. In this case they found an adult
dolphin, without any appearance of injury, but just
beached by the storm. There were enough air spaces
in the seaweed so that it could breathe, and the
dampness had kept it wet, shielding it from the air
and sun. They managed to get this dolphin, heavy
though it was, back into the water, and it seemed to
be all right and swam away.

Later, the two groups of people heard of each
other's adventures, and put it together. They
thought that the large dolphin may have been the
mother of the small one, since they were not far
apart, and must have been lost from one another in

the storm. We can imagine their happy reunion in the bay. Sonar sounds of both dolphins searching the waters anxiously, searching, searching, then *finding*, and rushing towards each other. Whistles and squeals, joyous leaps, fond nuzzlings and cuddlings, happy dashes and snuggles. Together again. I thought of how much easier it would be for them to find one another than for a human lost child and distressed mother, since these fortunate creatures have their sound/echo system to help them communicate and locate each other.

How nice to think that humans were able to help dolphins in distress on the land, as they so often help us in the sea. Our human gift to them this time.

Wilf commented on how the storm had indirectly caused Hazel to discover some new understanding. It seems that in the storm a prawn trawler had washed onto the beach at Monkey Mia, and in trying to rescue it, a bulldozer had become bogged in two meters of water at high tide! The dolphins had been enthusiastic spectators to all this marvelously interesting activity in their realm, and daily swam round and round the foundering machines investigating it all. Well, it was decided that the way to get the bulldozer dislodged was by blasting.

Hazel and Wilf were both horrified. The dolphins cannot be shooed away like chickens. Nor can they be led away and kept in a safe place like the curious children who lined the shore. Hazel found that she was very emotional about this. It was absolutely not going to happen, no matter how certain the engineers felt that it was necessary. She was ready to go out and bodily prevent such an occurence. The dolphins were *not* to be submitted to the possibility of such injury.

Well, another way was found, and the dozer was

removed without blasting. An interesting result,
however, was the discovery of Hazel's strong
feelings. It seems that she had been somewhat
critical of demonstrators reported in the news, such
as those opposing subdivision developers, for
example, who had placed their own bodies in front
of the bulldozers. Now she says she understands
how they feel. She was fully ready to lay her own
body down in the path of any blasting, and feels that
she knows what it means to be that dedicated to a
cause.

Returning from the trip to town, I find the tide
quite low, and dolphins are meeting a few human
friends at water's edge. There is nothing such as the
crowd of yesterday and Saturday. There's a brisk
cool breeze, so that it is chilling to stand in the
water; and at low tide there is not our usual smooth
sand under foot, but sticky mud to stand in, with
occasional sharp loose stones and bits of shell, not

at all pleasant. But the charm of the dolphins is such that their devotees endure this discomfort uncomplaining. It seems it would not be that pleasant for the dolphins either, for the water is murky, especially as the silt gets more and more stirred up from moving feet and thrashing dolphins. But they do not seem to mind at all.

As usual there are Nick, Puck, Holey-fin and little Joy. Some people have bought a package of the frozen yellowtails, which are being thawed at the water's edge. A little girl is holding one by the tail and dipping it over and over in the water as she has been shown to do to thaw it, and keeps asking, every few seconds, "Is it thawed now? Can I give it to them now?" Finally the fish is approved, and Nick glides in from the side, curving his body around to face the child. He raises his open beak out of the water and waits. The little one, now faced with actually getting *that* close to the rows of sharp looking teeth, is not so sure about this whole business. Gingerly she holds the fish at arm's length at least a farther arm's length from the waiting mouth. "Closer, Cynthia, you'll have to get closer." The child moves almost imperceptibly closer.

How many times this week have I seen this drama, eagerness and anxiety in conflict? Before the child can find the courage to approach closely enough, Nick closes his mouth, straightens out in the water and glides away. "Oh, it's *gone!*", wails the disappointed little girl.

"It will come back. Now just move in closer. It won't hurt you."

Next time around, with a little more encouragement from mum, the child manages to get the fish into the dolphin's mouth. A moment later Holey-fin is here for one too, and then Puck. Everyone is happy.

Later, at 3:00, the tide is in and the footing

more pleasant, and more dolphins have come. The
breeze has diminished a little too. It's a gorgeous
afternoon. Who are these other dolphins? There is
Crooked-fin, and B.B. swims past doing
simultaneous breathing close beside another
dolphin I do not recognize. Oh yes, it is that one I
have seen twice before with a slice out of the back
edge of the fin — A big heavy dark fellow. There is
something particularly pleasant about their
closeness as I watch them go past several times
fairly fast but in perfect synchronicity. B.B. comes
in for a fish and a pat, but the other one waits just
out of reach, watching quietly.

I get the feeling of a grown boy (B.B.) who has
brought home his new schoolmate to meet the
folks. They are accustomed to romping together in
wild abandonment, and sharing each other's every
thought and mood. But B.B. has this other whole
part of his life that is quite foreign to most dolphins.
From babyhood he has associated with humans. His
mother brought him here at least several times a
week, and often daily, except in the summer season.
They were here with Nick and his mother, and
Puck (a year younger) and his mother, who were all
accustomed to coming right in to shore to touch the
strange two-legged land creatures, and to take fish
from them. So B.B. has had this experience all his
life. The first two years, Old Speckledy Belly (their
grandmother, perhaps?) was also here constantly,
and was so gentle and friendly that she even allowed
the smallest humans to be placed on her back.

To B.B., all this is a natural, pleasant and
familiar game to play. But his new friend waits a
little apart, and only watches. One can imagine his
hesitant interest in seeing this daring activity
which his friend B.B. performs with perfect poise. Is
B.B. urging the friend to come and touch us? Are we
being told something about the friend? If so, it is a

pity that we have so little understanding. I would
love to know more about your friend, B.B., and
about your relationship. Will the day ever come
that I may know what you are saying?

All I can do now is talk to you in my own
language, and make absurd attempts to mimic your
squeals and clicks with my inadequate lips and
tongue. Perhaps these noises may sound ridiculous
to you, but I feel very confident that you do
understand my most important message: that I love
you and feel honored to have you here at my knees,
pushing your beak into my hand as I rub all around
the rubbery snout. I am perfectly confident that you
are aware of the deep affection that is meant to be
conveyed by my hand and voice and glance. It seems
of no importance that we are of different species,
arising from such different environments. We
know one another. We are aware of the loving
intentions on either side, of the earnest desire to be
in communion with one another.

I look out at the other dolphin poised at the edge of our warm exchange. It is evident that he is observing our every subtle move. Will he soon come in for a touch?

What is the attraction for them anyway? Why do the dolphins of Monkey Mia come into the very shallow water to be touched? And what is the attraction for us? Why does it seem so meaningful?

One of mankind's most pressing questions is always: "What does it all mean?" Do the dolphins also ponder such questions?

This afternoon the dolphins are in the mood for stroking. Nick and Puck and B.B., the three adolescents, come in again and again for a stroke along the side with the flat palm, and for vigorous chin rubs. There are two young boys wearing yellow T-shirts that say "Shark Bay" who appear to be brothers, perhaps nine and ten years old. They are

not at all shy or anxious in making friends with the dolphins, perhaps partly because they are a bit older than many of the children who come here, perhaps because they may have a somewhat different orientation to animals than some. They very quickly discover how best to approach the dolphin as it glides towards them, and what part of the face and body the dolphin likes to be stroked. They quickly pick up the name of each dolphin from those of us who are familiar, and within half an hour are relating to the dolphins as old friends.

I enjoy talking with them. They are from Manjimup (one of my favorite names among Australian towns! — last year at Eastertime, I went camping near there, south of Perth, in the magnificent forest of trees that are among the tallest in the world).

This family has no camera along, so I take a photograph with B.B. and offer to send it to them. But I strike a bargain: I will send it if Brad, the older boy, will write for me a little paper telling what he feels about his experience with the dolphins. I hope he does it.*

A little later there is another interesting group: three young adults, a woman and two men. They, too, fall right in to a close feeling of communion with the dolphins and seem to know exactly what approach will be most satisfying for both themselves and the dolphins. They quickly realize that it is easy to recognize one dolphin from another, and ask, "Do they have names?"

"Yes," I tell them, and ask the first man, "What is your name?"

"Stephen," he answers.

"Puck, this is Stephen," I address the dolphin. "Holey-fin, Stephen.

"How d'ya do," he responds, giving Holey a long

*He did. See the Postlogue.

lingering stroke along the side as she leans against
his hand in passing. In a few minutes they can tell
all the dolphins by name, and are scratching and
rubbing beaks, stroking sides and even getting in a
stroke for two dolphins simultaneously as Nick and
Puck come by together. It is a very mellow scene
today, with much clicking and squealing from the
dolphins. Are they also doing some introductions?
Are they saying to each other, "Let's call this one
Gloop, because his touch is so confident, and that
one Pleee because her voice is so pleasant"?

Today, as it has often been on other days, two or
three dolphins are holding court with a few
children at the far end of the beach, while a few
others are with us near the pier. Ringer stays with
one group for a little time, then when those
dolphins drift out to deeper water he looks
uncertainly at the other group. Finally he comes to
join the second group, but after a few minutes,
those dolphins go to see what the first group may
have to offer. Ringer, shivering from long hours in
the chilly water, gazes uncertainly down the beach,
then again shifts his position.

Then finally, when only he and I are left, Nick
and Puck come to be with us. The dog is standing
quite some distance from me, and the dolphins are
coming to him, rather than to me. I think of the fact
that dogs can hear the very high-frequency sounds
that dolphins make. I have heard of whistles people
blow to call dogs which the people themselves
cannot hear because they are of such high
frequency, but the dogs hear and respond readily. So
Ringer can hear the high-frequency sounds of the
dolphins that are inaudible to us, and is no doubt
aware of more dolphin talk than we are aware of.

Now each dolphin passes the dog slowly,
coming in a bit closer at each pass. Sometimes they
turn to face him, staying just under the surface of

the water. He is standing chest deep, so that the dolphin is facing his chest. Ringer is very intent and still, and it seems to me that the space between them is electric with messages. Finally Puck, after pausing this way in front of the dog, gently approaches more closely, still under water, and then . . . touches his beak to the dog's chest.

Ringer holds his head high, with eyes looking down in an ecstatic, breath-holding pause. Then Puck backs off and glides away.

Ringer is transfixed. Puck makes a turn with eye above water watching. Then he comes in again and repeats the gentle touch of beak to chest . . . and is gone. Ringer stands very still for a long moment, then blinks a few times, and seems to relax.

A lovely scene. Now what do you suppose they conveyed to each other?

Several dolphins are playing out in the deeper water with tiny Joy discernible among them. The three adolescents, B.B., Puck and Nick, plus B.B.'s friend, are staying more with the shore people, but make excursions out to where the others are cavorting. They are too far out for me to identify them. A man on shore is sitting on his truck and taking some movie films from up high enough to get a good view. "They should come out quite well," I comment to him. "They are giving a real show today." He smiles. "Actually I doubt that the film will amount to much. They are quite far out. But when I watch the film at home, it will remind me of what great fun it was to be here watching them."

The dolphins leap out of the water in unison, three and even four abreast. They leapfrog over one another, dive and disappear, then suddenly come hurtling up out of the water chasing one another.

Joy does her little half-turn leap, re-entering the
water upside down. Once or twice one dolphin will
stand on its tail, hovering above the water wriggling
slightly. It is clear that no dolphin needs a human to
teach it to put on a show.

As the afternoon wanes, the excitement also
subsides, and fewer dolphins are to be seen. Finally
there are none in sight, as the sun sinks. I have
noticed that the pattern I observed last year does
not seem to hold true for this year. They do not all
disappear at once. Hazel had said at the time that
she did not think that was really very typical,
except for the particular time I had happened to be
here.

In the evening Hazel and daughter Jenny come
to my caravan and we have a cup of tea together.
"You'll be leaving tomorrow, and we've hardly had
time to see you! We haven't even had a yoga lesson,"
exclaims Hazel. "Yes, you have been *so* busy. It is
such a pity that the only time I could come here is
when you would be so tied up."

"Can we have a lesson in the morning?" Hazel
asks. And Jenny says she and her husband would
also like to join in. So we agree on an early morning
session, before the demands of the campground
need to be met.

We talk a little about the planned foundation
for protecting the dolphins, and for providing
information about dolphins to visitors who come
with no preparation and find themselves feeding
and petting a creature that seems much the same as
a fish, though they vaguely know it is not.

Wilf and Hazel are both a bit haunted by the
thought that something could happen and that the
dolphins might cease to come any more. What
would them be done with any funds that had
accumulated for the dolphin foundation? There
could be a provision that funds could be used for

other human-dolphin contacts elsewhere in
Australia, or for general education about dolphins.

How much do the dolphins here need to be
protected? Does anyone try to harm them? Have
there been any dolphin deaths, other than Old
Charley? Hazel said, "We believe Old Speckledy
Belly is dead, because we have not seen her for three
years, and we cannot imagine anything else
preventing her from coming. We assume she died a
natural death, because she seemed to be old. Of
course we do not *know* that she was a *she,* we just
felt that to be so.

"There have been three bodies of baby dolphins
found. One was found in a net that was set in the
channel east of the jetty about the end of the first
year we were here. Then the second year, two baby
dolphins were found badly cut up, both about the
head. We suspected that they had been playing
under fast moving boats in deep water, and as the
boats passed from deep to shallow water, the
dolphins were hit. None of these were dolphins that
we had come to know here at the beach.

The information about these little dolphins
was used by the local Fisheries Inspector when he
applied for a speed limit to be placed on boats in the
area and to prohibit nets within 800 meters of this
beach where they come to see us. So we owe the
protection we have for our dolphins to these deaths.

"There was one other body found, and that was
a sad story," Hazel said. "One day a new dolphin
came to me at the beach. It came straight to me,
without any hesitation, as I was feeding the
regulars. I was struck by the strangeness of that.
Usually a new dolphin will dally around for a long
time, weeks or months, before finally coming in to
take a fish or be touched, but this one swam straight
in, and right up to me. It was making a sound I had
never heard before, and it sounded to me that it was

crying. I was feeding the others, and I offered this one a fish. It took it, but the fish fell right out of its mouth. I tried several times, but the dolphin couldn't seem to hold the fish. And it kept making that sound. I told Wilf, 'there's a dolphin down there that I'm sure is crying. I can't make out what is the matter, but it can't seem to eat.' Then later a dolphin body was found on the beach, and we thought it was the same one. The fisheries man said it had a broken jaw. Some of the campers said that the jaw had been shot, but that is only hearsay. We have never seen anyone take a gun to the dolphins. However it happened, the dolphin had a broken jaw, and could not hold a fish to eat. I have felt so touched to think that it came to us for help, and so sad that there was nothing I could do."

What do you suppose those dolphins say to one another out there in the sea? "There are some strange creatures in there at Monkey Mia who dangle fish at the surface while we take them in our mouths. Perhaps they can help you, O poor friend with a broken jaw."

I had been reading a passage in the Encyclopedia of Australian Fisheries telling of the social organization of dolphins, according to an unnamed observer. It said that bottlenosed dolphins live in herds of females and young with a mature bull as head, while young males roam alone or in groups. But that when a young male approaches the herd, the dominant male does not drive him off, and does not even prevent him from consorting with the females of the herd. It seems so sensible. Hazel and Jenny and I discussed it. We mused over whether any of those dolphins we see farther out in the water might be the Big Boy. And are all these who come nearer females and young? The six regulars who let us touch them are indeed three mothers and their three adolescent offspring. How about B.B.'s new friend? And Rags, and Notch and Sickle-fin? Are they more females, or are some of them young males? Or even older ones? "Is this a nursery, here at Monkey Mia?" Hazel asks. "Wilf and I have wondered about that before. Will we ever know?" I wonder, too.

Tuesday 2 September 80

6:00. The indigo sky is strewn with sparkling diamonds that seem to lose none of their brilliance as the background lightens to royal blue. A deep red flushes the east. A lone fisherman with pole is silhouetted aginst the flaming glow there at the end of the dock.

No dolphins yet.

It is my last day. I must pack. How brief the time has seemed.

After a very pleasant yoga lesson in the Mason's comfortable big living room, I go out to find Nick and Puck taking pats from some children. Crooked-fin is playing with little Joy close out, and Holey-fin is farther to the left, inspecting some boats that have just been drawn up on the sand. I give a few long strokes to Nick and then to Puck as

they glide close to me. They often come together, and I can rub both beaks at the same time, one with each hand. Then Holey-fin comes to rub against my shins, as I stroke her farther side, so that her big body is between my legs and my hand as she slides through. She comes back and takes my fingers softly in her mouth, the little sharp teeth tickling. "Hello, Holey. You are feeling affectionate for so early in the morning. Do you know that I must leave today?" She comes for another turn. Then Puck again, for a very long slow rub from my palm against his side. Nick crowds him and I pet them both. Nick comes for a two-hand stroke, one palm on each of his sides, pressing hard against the strong solid body. Now Crooked-fin is here, with open beak. "Sorry, lady, but I have no fish," I tell her, as I scratch her beak all over. All of them are making the soft Oooo Oooo Oooo sound on a descending note.

I could do this all day, but must go and pack.

11:00. I can't resist going out to see what my marine friends are doing. Nick and Puck and B.B. are taking fish from a newly arrived family. Father and mother stand on the sand, while a little girl and smaller boy stand in the water. The girl has become confident enough to hold the fish where the dolphins can reach them while the father photographs. The little boy shrinks behind her each time the dolphin approaches near. Once, as Nick is taking a fish, B.B. comes around behind the girl and gently nudges the boy's small hand. I notice that B.B. keeps his beak closed, and the little fellow's face relaxes into a smile as the dolphin drifts away. The boy looks up at his mother with a delighted glance.

"Wasn't that nice, James?" the mother says. "The dolphin came in specially to you. You see how sweet they are?" The mother takes off her shoes and wades into the water as well. Soon the father joins them, and Holey-fin comes for her share of the feed. The bucket of fish is soon emptied, and the dolphins stay to be petted. The whole family is entranced.

"Oh, look at the baby!" says the girl, noticing Joy for the first time. "What a darling. Oh, Mother, do you think I can pet it as well?" But Joy stays beyond reach. Once as Holey-fin and Joy are passing, only two meters out, it can easily be seen that Joy is suckling. I point this out to the family, who are enchanted with the sight, and eager to learn more about the dolphin physiology. I share the facts I have recently acquired about how the milk is very thick, more like the consistency of cottage cheese, and that the mother can squirt it out into the baby's mouth.

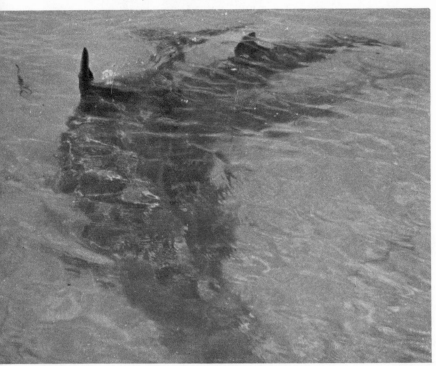

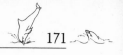

Reluctantly, back to my caravan I go, to continue making some order of all the papers and to check the drying of clothing on the line.

At 1:00 I am at the beach again, and there are a large number of dolphins at varying distances from shore, engaged in different sorts of play. Crooked-fin, Nick and Puck are seeking pats from some children. B.B. is cruising back and forth with his new friend of the other day, about three meters out. Farther out I can recognize tiny Joy among several other dolphins who are lazily cruising and surfacing to breathe. Very far out, another dolphin or two occasionally surfaces.

When I wade into the water, Puck comes to me lifting beak out of the water for a chin scratch, softly oooo-ing. He returns several times, gathering speed, faster and with more vigor each turn, as I catch him quickly under the beak on each pass, and give him a stroke down the side. Then on one pass, as I grasp under his beak, he suddenly flips over in a somersault, using my hand as a base! SPLASH, he comes down in the water on his back, quickly twists onto his usual belly position, and glides away with one eye out of the water, regarding my astonishment. What fun! There is no end to the little surprises these dolphins have for us.

B.B. and Nick and Holey-fin come to see what is going on, and all engage in fast games of chase and tumble, with B.B.'s friend joining in, and soon Crooked-fin and Joy as well. A short distance out I can see Rags and Notch. And soon, when most of the bunch head out deeper, another dolphin comes to glide past the shore about four meters out. It has a more curved back edge to the fin than most, and I recognize it as the one I had called Sickle-fin. Everyone is here today. Except . . , I realize that I never did see the new dolphin Wilf had named Snubnose. Gosh, fellows, I'll never get packed. And

I have no more film to photograph the fins of these
dolphins who have showed themselves so seldom.

Back to the caravan to finish getting things
packed. When at last it is all done, and I load my
things into the car of the people who have offered
me a ride to Denham, I go down to the shore for a
last fond look. Fortunately the people are ready to
drive away and I cannot take much time to linger
sentimentally. There they all are: Holey-fin and Joy,
Nick and Puck, coming for pats from children and
an adult at the shore. Ringer is there, of course.
Crooked-fin and B.B. with some other dolphin are a
little farther out. And here is sleek, pale Beautiful,
with her feather scar, gliding past with one eye
tilted out. Goodbye, dear Beautiful. As I watch her
looking at me, I get the notion that the next time I
see her it will be with another new baby!Interesting
that that thought should come to me, because I had
not thought that I might see my dolphin friends
again any time soon, but feel at this moment that I
shall. Did you send that message to me, Beautiful? I
stand quietly for a few seconds in that blankness
that I so often have experienced with the dolphins,
gazing into Beautiful's eye.

Turning finally to leave, I meet one of the
children coming out of the water, who says to me,
"Did you see how many there are? We counted
fifteen." I turn for a last look. Yes, there are eight in
close, and four in the middle distance, and at least
three more father out.

Thank you, dear dolphins, for your gift of
friendship offered to me during these days I have
spent here at your beach. I hope you know that I
admire your graceful happy life, and how joyfully
you live together with each other and how
forthrightly you come to share it with us as well.
Please accept my offer of love in return. May I

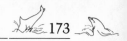
understand your meaning in whatever way it is possible for me.

Goodbye to Wilf and Hazel, who leave customers standing in the busy shop to come out and hug me. We'll write to one another.

The ride along the red dirt road among the carpets of wildflowers, making conversation, seems unreal. In Denham I say goodbye to Jan and Lee Ann and Barry in the Post Office store. Tony drives me the long road to the bus, because he needs to pick up supplies for his little fast-food bar. Everyone is exhausted from the crowds of tourists in their usually quiet little town. But it will end very soon now.

I have a slight sense of *deja vu* as I have another cup of hot chocolate with a cheese sandwich in the roadhouse, this time with Tony. Then the big bus is here. I hug Tony and climb aboard, engulfed suddenly with a wave of the lovely perfume of the acacia blossoms blown by the wind from across the land. Goodbye.

Riding throught the night, I drift into my dolphin consciousness. Deep quiet watery oneness. Quiet companionable joyfulness.
All-encompassing dolphin deepness. Surging flowing powerful muscularness. Flowing curving plunging gracefulness. Forever everywhere oneness in dolphinness.

7

Learning More About Dolphins

Within two weeks I was back in California, and, eager to find out more of what others had learned about dolphins, I began contacting some organizations that concern themselves with cetaceans. I met Stan and Ken Minasian of the Marine Mammal Fund, and devoured their booklet called *Dolphins,* a most concise and easily understood collection of facts about dolphins. I met Pieter Folkens, the artist who did the beautiful cover of that booklet: two dolphins as seen from deep within the water, hanging suspended and weightless, gracefully nudging one another, conveying the three dimensional quality of movement in the water. The Marine Mammal Fund is a non-profit organization for research and education to help the public know more of what our sea-dwelling cousins are like, so that we may stop our violence to them. Their new book, *The World's Whales,* will be off the press soon. This big handsome book will be a definitive atlas of all dolphins and whales, with 200 beautiful illustrations. They were excited to tell me one day that they had received a photograph from China of the freshwater dolphin that lives in a lake there, to add to the collection of rare illustrations in the book.

I also contacted the Northern California office of Greenpeace and was invited to show my slides of the

Monkey Mia dolphins and tell about them. They had never heard of a whole family of dolphins who came freely to shallow water to meet humans. We scheduled this presentation for lunch time so that people could come from their jobs. I was most impressed to see so many make the effort to come, and their interest was gratifying. As one said to me, "After years of combatting the killing of dolphins and whales, wading around in blood as it were, how rewarding it is to see this Monkey Mia demonstration of humans and dolphins getting along so happily together." It is a beginning of how the dolphins will reward our efforts with the gift of their friendship. The Greenpeace staff asked to use a few of my slides regularly in presentations they make to the public, so I had copies made for them.

Birgit Winning of the Steinhart Aquarium staff asked to include some of the Monkey Mia slides in a presentation she was making to the Aquarium Society at the Academy of Sciences in San Francisco, and invited me to speak to the audience myself about my slides. It was fun to hear the gasps of pleasure as they saw children petting wild dolphins, and the dog Ringer gazing into Puck's eye.

Ken Minasian had been to visit the laboratory where John C. Lilly's organization, the Human/Dolphin Foundation, is doing some research on communication between the two species. Ken had taken a swim there, playing with some dolphins, and when he started to get out of the pool, one dolphin was not ready to end the frolic. As he was about to hoist himself out of the pool, Ken was startled to find a powerful bundle of muscles insistently pushing against him as a flipper grasped him under the arm! So he had to take time for another bit of stroking before he was allowed to clamber out! It is nice to develop such a close friendship so quickly, and a good lesson in how determined a dolphin can be to get its strokes. Ken told Dr. Lilly and his wife, Antonietta, about Monkey Mia, and brought back an invitation for me to present my slide show to them and their staff. I looked forward to meeting this famous scientist and learning more about the new project,

wondering if it might shed some light on communicating with our dolphins.

I asked everyone about encounters with other dolphins, and found that reports of someone actually touching a wild dolphin are fairly rare. There was one other dolphin similar to Donald (the one reported in *Follow a Wild Dolphin*). This one appeared in a bay in Spain, made friends with a diver, and became as popular as Opo. Although it did not meet its admirers at the beach the way Opo did, crowds of tourists thronged the small seaside town of La Corogna to see the dolphin frolicking daily out in the bay. The dolphin was called "Nina", the Spanish word meaning literally "baby", but often used as a term of endearment, as we sometimes use it in English. This "baby" was about eight feet long weighing some 400 pounds, and would come right up to any one of several divers she recognized, to swim with him and be carressed. Like Opo and Donald, she would not take fish from the men, but caught her own food. Laws were enacted to protect the popular animal, prohibiting the use of outboard motors near her and forbidding nets in the cove.

Funds were raised to build a monument to her. But after a
few months she failed to appear as usual, and her body was
found, apparently the victim of an explosion.

Another report I read tells of the dolphin "Dolly" who
adopted a family in the Florida Keys. This dolphin would
appear daily at their small dock in a canal that wound
some distance inland from the open sea, and the children
would swim with her. The mother of the family would
talk with her and feed her fish, and the dolphin would
squeak and whistle and do tricks to please her human
friends.

One game they enjoyed playing was with a handful of
coins. The woman would throw into the water some coins
of mixed denominations — pennies, nickles and dimes —
and tell Dolly to retrieve only the dimes. Now this water
was murky, and the bottom was so muddy that the coins
sank into the silt. Humans who tried were unable to find
any coins. But the dolphin unfailingly found and brought
back all the dimes, which are made of silver, and never any
of the lesser coins, which are so nearly the same size but
are made of copper and nickle respectively. This is a fine
example of the precision of the dolphin's echo-location
capability.

It was learned that this dolphin had been captured and
trained by the Navy at a nearby center but had been freed
because she was considered unsuitable for their purposes.
Apparently she missed her human contact, and perhaps
she was not able to find a dolphin family at sea with whom
to make a satisfactory bond. The human family enjoyed
her for quite some time, but her rather insistant demands
for attention eventually became difficult, and she was
taken to a dolphinarium to live.

It became clear to me that there are several ways in
which the dolphin phenomenon at Monkey Mia is different from all the other accounts I have been able to find.
First, our dolphins come into the shallow water for their
human contacts, and otherwise only Opo has done that.
Second, there is a whole group of dolphins, not just a single

one. Third, none of these dolphins has ever been captured, so the initiative is entirely the dolphins'. Fourth, they take food offered by hand, and not only accept but actually seek stroking, even from humans they have never seen before. Fifth, they bring their babies to the immediate vicinity of the human presence. And last, they have been visiting at the beach regularly for some sixteen years!

Seeing how much interest there was in the Monkey Mia phenomenon, Mark Allen of Whatever Publishing (they published my first yoga book) urged me to go ahead and write a book about the dolphins, using as the heart of the book the journal I had kept while there. The Masons and I had talked earnestly about whether it would be harmful to the dolphins to publicize their friendship with humans, and to reveal the location of Monkey Mia. For some time now, however, an Australian government brochure for tourists has shown a picture of their beach at Monkey Mia with dolphins being fed by hand, so it is no secret. And, as we saw this year, quite a number of families driving on holiday in Western Australia do come out the peninsula just to see the dolphins. The long rough dirt road has been some deterrent, but new surfacing will be completed soon, and surely more tourists will then be willing to make the diversion. There *will* be more crowds to visit the dolphins. But Wilf and Hazel had felt that they were prepared for this because they had succeeded in getting the government protection they had sought, and if more were needed, they believe their requests would be heeded. Also, we all felt that Monkey Mia is still remote. It would not be like telling all these Americans (who are reading this book) about a dolphin beach near Sydney, for example, where it would be easy to take a half-day expedition during one's two-week tour of Hawaii, New Zealand and Australia! Perth is a long and expensive air trip from Sydney, and Shark Bay is still 800 kilometers beyond Perth. Going out the peninsula to Monkey Mia is still a long detour, even if it is paved and can be traveled more quickly. For all these reasons, it doesn't seem that our dolphins will be inundated with American tourists.

I wrote the Masons about the prospective book, telling them that part of the royalties would go to help support their new dolphin protection foundation. They responded that they believe it is the right time for the world
to learn about the dolphins there, and that it is a beautiful
experience to have their friendship. We decided to go
ahead with the book.

As I began to be introduced at gatherings as someone
writing a book about dolphins, now and then I met people
who would tell me of their experiences with dolphins, or
the experiences of someone they knew. One young woman
told me about her childhood memories of her father relating histories of Navy service in World War II. He said
sailors always prayed that if they were shipwrecked, dolphins might be nearby, because they knew dolphins would
help them to shore. He told the children of Navy friends
who had been helped by dolphins to stay afloat through
long miserable hours of dark wet wandering, then had
been nudged through dangerous shoals to a dawn landing
on a safe beach. When I asked eagerly in what seas this had
taken place, she did not know, and now her father is
deceased. But she has a lifelong image of dolphins as
warm, intelligent, life-saving creatures who care about the
welfare of humans.

One can imagine the experience of both the men and
the dolphins during these agonizing times. — The explo-
sions with their cataclysmic sounds, the sudden horrible
compression in the water that the dolphins would have
felt, the blinding brilliance, the heat, then objects flying
about and falling in the water, oil spreading, tasting horrid,
and perhaps getting into the blowhole when the dolphin
came up to breathe, possibly catching fire and spreading
flames over the surface of the sea! Then strange warm
bodies floundering in the water, probably shouting, distressed.

And the dolphins' response: through all the terror and
turmoil, a fellow creature needing help. Those strange

creatures who *can* swim, but not very well, and who tire so easily. Who seem intelligent, but do such weird things (all that fire and brokenness and death). No question but to help. They have to get to land. They live more easily on the land. And so they are helped to shore.

Another young woman I met, Lin Fox, told me of having a dolphin friend in Hawaii about six years ago. Ahiku was a young male dolphin, one of those used in a research project by the Navy at Kaneohe Bay. A marine biologist there was a friend of this woman and for two or three months he used to take her to visit the dolphin every Saturday. The dolphin lived in a watery pen, but there was a flap door, she said, that allowed him to come and go at will out into the open bay. He became accustomed to her visits and would never be absent when she came. He would show great excitement when he saw her approaching down the long pier. "He would be flipping around and talking and standing on his tail. First, I would feed him, and as he jumped up to take the fish from my hand, each time he would brush his beak caressingly against my palm before grasping the fish from my fingers. Then I would get in the water and swim with him for an hour."

We talked about how it feels to be examined with dolphin sonar. Those clicks that you hear on the sound track of dolphin films are not something I have ever heard, and she said she also had not heard the sonar, but rather she had *felt* it. "It is a sensation of almost a caressing vibration all through the body, a very pleasant sensation," she said. "I would float on my back and he would come up under me, belly up, and slide along against me from my feet up my legs and back. His skin was silky, and it was very sensuous. It was all very happy. I feel that the connection is still very much alive, not fading in memory at all. I know I will always feel him with me and caring for me." We talked about the complete openness of the dolphin relationship, as nearly everyone feels it. Total acceptance. She said, "With the dolphin I would get an opportunity to drop the weight of my human limitations and feel free."

She said her seven year old daughter had a friendship at the same time with a young female dolphin there named Suzy, with whom she would play in the water. The child was an excellent swimmer, and would hug the dolphin and the two of them would roll around and frolic and dive in the water together. The mother was happy for her child to have this relationship with the joyous animal. Of her own experience she said, "It was a wonderful relationship. I felt more close to him emotionally, and more in harmony with his male energy, than I ever have to any person."

Several persons I met told me of incidents when a dolphin, or several, would appear in the waves beside them when they were surfing, and would expertly ride the curling wave, their lithe bodies showing clearly in the green water. One said he shared his sport with a particular dolphin for two hours. Every time he made his way back out to deep water after riding a wave into shore, the dolphin would appear again beside him with a bright appreciative eye, and the man learned to watch the dolphin for the exact moment and position to take the wave for a fine ride, taking cues from a real pro.

Others that I met would tell me of their dreams of dolphins and whales. It seems that many who have never seen a dolphin, even in a sea circus, have regular dreams about them, and sometimes receive advice or guidance from their dream dolphins or whales, much in the manner of the Delphic oracle of old.

One day as I was parking my car in front of a building where I had an appointment, I noticed that another car there had a small dolphin painted on the fender. I thought that I was destined to meet someone inside who had a common interest with me. It turned out that I was introduced to a young woman by the name of Deon Dolphin, and she told me her story. Her parents named her Deon, but the surname she adopted. It seems that one day she was meditating with a friend, and was in a particularly deep and profound quietness for a very long time. When she finally opened her eyes, her friend was watching her with an astonished look. "You just had a dolphin in the middle of your forehead," the friend exclaimed.

Deon felt that she would like to take the name of Dolphin, but was not sure if she had a right to do that. She decided to ask permission. She went to the Steinhart Aquarium to the dolphin tank there, and walked up to the plate-glass window. A dolphin was in the far corner. She spoke to the dolphin, and asked if it would be all right for her to call herself "Deon Dolphin." She says the dolphin told her it would be all right if she would live up to it. That answer seemed good to her. But she told the dolphin, "I want a little more confirmation than that. You are hiding way over there in the corner." And at that the dolphin swam over to the glass and pressed her beak against the window and looked into Deon's eyes for a good long time, so she felt satisfied. She has used her new name ever since, and feels that she is basing her life on principles of harmony, joy and compassion that she attributes to dolphins.

Another person I met was Rose Farrington, an initiator of the New Games movement. These are games designed to encourage people to play together creatively, with harmony and joy, and without anyone "losing" the game. In these games everyone contributes in their own way as the action of the game evolves, and everyone "wins" just by being in the game.

She told me of how it came about that she first had ideas for these games. It was in 1973 in San Francisco, and she had been feeling very discouraged about the state of the world and of the human race, with all the violence, and hunger, and drug abuse, and environmental pollution, and corruption in government. One grey foggy Sunday, in a matching grey mood, she walked into the Steinhart Aquarium. As she came down a dim corridor with lighted fish tanks on either side, she saw at the end a huge plate glass window giving view into the side of a tank that is open to the sky above. It was at that time populated with three dolphins. She stood at the rail watching through the glass.

"I saw the grey and white flashes of the graceful creatures of the sea," she wrote of her experience. "Suddenly I
was beyond the rail, leaning my anguished face against the
cold panel of glass. I thought how inhumane we humans
are. 'You beautiful creatures, don't men understand that
they have separated you from your families? They pen you
up, feed you dead fish, and view you as curiosities.' Grief
wracked my body.

"Then words began to flow back into my mind. 'We
are ambassadors from the sea.' The three dolphins began
sliding their bodies against the glass where my face
was . . .' we are love and cooperation . . . play is the answer
you are looking for . . . ' One of the dolphins rose gracefully
to the surface and brought back an eighteen inch piece of
orange yarn, and began to dive, glide and twist, while the
piece of yarn danced on flipper, tail, beak and body.

"Joy began to pulse inside me. I laughed and clapped
my hands at the delicious creature's play. A second dolphin joined the game, and then the third. The three dolphins romped in the water forming patterns, then changing them. Words came to me. ' . . . bring people together . . . play together . . . cooperate . . . play . . . peace on
the planet . . . '

"I was deeply changed, radiant and hopeful, full of
energy, shooting synapses through my nervous system
with joyful explosion."

She went away and thought often about what she had
experienced, spoke about it with many friends, and began
to form plans for using her new ideas. Two months later
she was hired by the producers of the Whole Earth
Catalogue to help organize the first New Games Tourna-
ment. This event took place in October, 1973 at Marin
Headlands, and was a tremendous success.

She says, "We bring people together to play coopera-
tively, erasing if only for a brief time all barriers of race,
age, sex, size, ability, socio-economic background, belief
structure. Creating the rules begins the game, choice and

freedom get activitated, then there is spontaneous group interaction where laughter dances over fields of grass and skips high into the trees, teeth flashing, hair flying, an earth-choreographed dance of expressive bodies. There are shouts of surprise and delight, each person a part of the game's magical body. Everybody plays, everybody wins. They share a common experience, but retain individuality. Each person has much to contribute to the group, and cooperation creates a gentle forum for personal participation, realizing one's own strength and sharing that.

"It can be a design for future living: individuals coming together from personal strength to a cooperative process for the generation of a quality shared experience.

"I played with the theories, testing them in systems: education, community organizing, business, government. My world was filled with pictures of groups of smiling people, actively participating, differences celebrated and shared, information developed on how to create positive solutions.

"I began to realize that I was learning from the dolphins a form that unites people, who then create a positive electrical field that appears to attract more people, in a comfortable space by-passing the usual initial awkwardness of interaction. It is a process that we can carry with us — to the back yard, to a meeting, to a picnic — in our minds. Simple games that can start with one person and expand to include hundreds."

She was invited to an international community education conference in Mexico in 1975, where the new games attracted much interest. From there she was employed to go to Australia, where she shared her new approach, and now hundreds of thousands of people in many countries have enjoyed this lively and nourishing experience of discovery. All beginning with some dolphins at play together with a piece of yarn.

She says, "In the years that have followed, New Games grew and spread and evolved. Microscopic worlds of graceful interaction, smiles, hugs, and peace in action.

The dolphins and I talk often. We celebrate the small: inspiration, commitment, and joy for the continued task, the realization that we are one family on earth."

One most intriguing person I met was Jim Nollman, a man who plays music to animals, he and they responding to one another, each with their own sounds. He played a flute to turkeys who would come to dance and gobble in response. He listened to morning and evening "songs" of timber wolves and played harmony with them on wind instruments.

He has played to grey whales, dolphins and orcas, using everything from an ancient lute to conventional instruments to special ones built to play underwater.

They responded beautifully, and he to them also, as they taught him phrases! He says they were communicating "the energy exchange of harmony." It was inspiring to talk with this congenial person who is active in creating more conscious relations between humans and animals.

His organization, Interspecies Communication, is using sound to help separate dolphins from fishermen in various parts of the world, a most hopeful solution to that conflict.

It was fascinating to discover these very different kinds of connections that various individuals have found with dolphins and other cetaceans. Fascinating, too, was all the literature. I felt I needed to learn more about the research that has been taking place with dolphins, and proceeded to read all I could find, and to talk with as many knowledgeable people as I could corner. It has illuminated a marvelous new world for me. Much of what I learned has helped me to understand what had been happening at Monkey Mia.

One of the first books I read was *Mind in the Waters*, aptly subtitled *A Book to Celebrate the Consciousness of Whales and Dolphins*. It is a collection of writings gathered by Joan McIntyre, and includes poetry and inspirational personal experiences as well as much careful scientific explanation.

For example, I learned that when the dolphin is facing directly towards us as we stand in the shallow water, it cannot see us with its eyes because there is a blind area directly ahead and *above*. It *can* see straight ahead and *below*, so it can see our feet with both eyes (binocular vision), but not up into our face. It must turn its head to one side and look up with one eye (monocular vision), to see the fish we would hold out to it. Often the visitors to

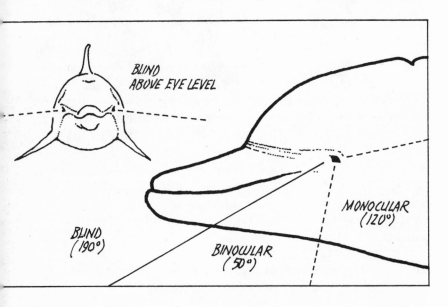

Monkey Mia would hold the fish higher and higher to try to get more of the head out of the water for a photograph, while I noticed that the dolphin much preferred to have the fish given to it *in* the water. When they opened their beaks as they approached us, the lower jaw would be just under the surface of the water, and therefor the eyes, which are on a line with the corner of the mouth, would also be just submerged. I noticed this especially, because I too was trying to get a good photograph of the whole head showing the eyes. Only when Nick or Puck or one of the others were doing their reconnoitering act, cruising back and forth tilted to one side, would we get a good view of the one eye out of the water, but not when we were seeing them head on.

I learned also something about how dolphins make their sounds. There are air cavities in the dolphin's head, just under the blowhole, and with the blowhole closed the dolphin can force air through a stretched opening from one cavity to the other to make a sound much as we make when we stretch the mouth of a balloon and allow the air to squeeze out. This accounts for why I could not see any movement of the blowhole when Nick would be cooing his "Oooo Oooo Oooo" to me. It is necessary for humans (and most animals) to let air escape in order to make sounds, but the dolphin (and other cetaceans) can make sounds while keeping the air inside. It *can* also make sounds by letting air escape: The whistling sounds seem to be accompanied by air bubbles from the blowhole when the dolphin is underwater. There is also another kind of sound that captive dolphins make, which seems to be learned in attempts to communicate with humans, made by vibrating the blowhole cover as air escapes. It sounds like a "Bronx cheer", a sound used by saucy children to indicate great disrespect and defiance. We used to make it by sticking out our tongues and blowing gently to vibrate

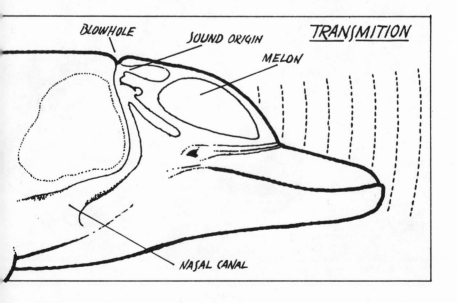

BLOWHOLE   SOUND ORIGIN   MELON   TRANSMITION

NASAL CANAL

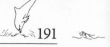
the lower lip against the tongue. I am sure everyone can remember doing this toward the retreating back of some parent or teacher or other authority who had just ordered us to do something we did not want to do. Dolphins do this very well, but I do not have the impression it has anything like the emotional charge that human children are expressing. Although perhaps the dolphins *are* razzing their trainers. They would certainly be justified in having such feelings toward the humans who keep them captive. Or it may be they are just trying to make a greater variety of sounds audible to humans, in response to our attempts to establish verbal communication. I never heard the dolphins at Monkey Mia make such sounds.

The echo-location impulses are sent out from the domed forehead, and in this position the dolphin is showering us with a rapid fire of little sounds that register in the dolphin's mind as a picture. Now this picture is of not only the surface of the object the dolphin is facing. It is more like an x-ray, or even more like the moving fluoroscope picture we see of our foot in a shoe store. It is a picture in depth. A dolphin "sonaring" a diver can see not only our

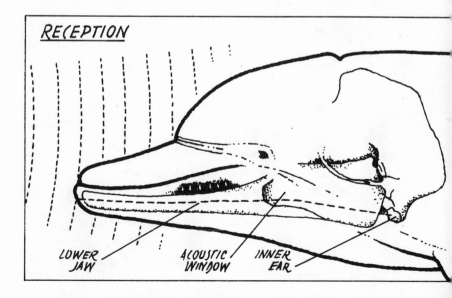

RECEPTION

LOWER JAW   ACOUSTIC WINDOW   INNER EAR

outside contours, but also our skeleton. It can see our
heart beating, our lungs breathing in and out, the blood
coursing through our veins, the state of our digestion, how
our glands are functioning. Imagine! No secrets from
these fellows.

Do you remember one of the childhood heroes who
had x-ray eyes? It was supposed to enable him to see
through walls, I believe. But I do not remember that it was
indicated that he could see into his friends' bodies and be
aware of their physiological state.

The dolphins have no need of a bio-feedback laboratory. If I had their ability I could look at my own arm and see
the condition of my blood pressure without need of the
cuff the doctor uses. What an aid to health it would be. No
need for all the tests conducted by elaborate machinery.
Just glance at the body and see what is happening.

Imagine how strange it would be to them if they could
understand that we can *not* see this way. (*Do* they understand this about us?) Poor limited creatures who can see
only the surface of things. We have made up for some of
our limitations by inventing a myriad of machines and
gadgets to perform some of these miracles. The dolphins,
with many millions of years of evolution behind them,
have developed these abilities within their own body and
nervous system. Given a few more millions of years, will
we be able to dispense with our gadgets and have the
abilities within ourselves?

It is said that dolphins cannot use their echo-location
system in the air, but only in water. I have wondered about
this, because it did seem to me that the dolphins had a
strong sense of us when we were standing above and in
front of them, where their eyes cannot see us (see page   ),
and where they could not sonar unless they could use it in
air. Bats use their echo-location in air, why not dolphins? I
inquired of a physicist. I was told that the sounds would
travel at a different speed in the air, and the reception of
the echoes would then have to be processed differently.
Perhaps that is too much of a change for a dolphin to cope

with, but it seems that it might be _possible_ for dolphins to learn that.*

I read Fichtelius' and Sjolander's fascinating book called _Smarter than Man?_ in which these Swedish scientists compared the intelligence of humans and cetaceans. They commented that we do not know exactly what whales use their large brains for, but they make the point that they must be used for something or they would not have evolved. On the other hand, in David and Melba Caldwell's book, _The World of the Bottlenosed Dolphin_, they compare the dolphin's intelligence with that of the dog and feel that there is not much difference. I notice that the "world of the dolphin" in their book is in a dolphinarium. I very much doubt that any dolphin would agree that a concrete tank with a few other dolphins, and an occasional human, constitutes his "world." What a sensory deprivation it must be for a dolphin to be put in this sterile environment, where there is so little underwater scenery and activity for the sonar to reveal, and no seaweed, no skittering schools of fishes, no tides and ocean waves. A very different "world" indeed.

Still, there is much of interest in the book. They commented that among dolphins some older females developed spotting on the underside. Old Speckledly Belly had these markings. Holey-fin now has such spots, like brown freckles on an otherwise grey dolphin. Does this mean that she is growing old?

In reading I found several observers commenting that dolphins engage in considerable sensuous sex activity that is not necessarily related to reproduction, much as humans do, but with considerably less self-consciousness.

Dolphins frequently nuzzle one another at the genital slit, similar to the way dogs do as a greeting and in getting acquainted. Dogs are strongly oriented to their sense of smell, and so they sniff at one another. Dolphins have no sense of smell, but explore one another with a shower of little echo-clicks.

Love play among dolphins is prolonged and graceful,

*One big difference is that bats have ears to catch sounds travelling in air, while dolphins receive waterbourne sounds through the lower jaw!

sometimes languid, sometimes intense, as they chase and entertwine with one another, stroke with their flippers, nibble and nuzzle. Copulation takes place often with the female in her normal swimming position at the water's surface, while the male approaches upside down from underneath, but a variety of other positions are also used. The female often initiates sexual play as well as the male, and not only when the female is in estrus, but at any time for sensual pleasure.

Sexual arousal seems to accompany much of their ordinary play, and satisfaction is reached whether between adult male and female, or between any combination of ages and genders, beginning in infancy. (They say a baby male dolphin gets an erection at only a few weeks old, and is taught by his mother and aunties how to enjoy it. How different from our typical shocked reaction!) Male/male relations are engaged in, or female/female, or dolphin/ human, or dolphin/sea turtle, or dolphin with a floating oar from a row-boat or with almost any other object that could possibly be found to be sensuously stimulating.

I am somewhat amused to recall that I have heard on several occaions the claim that one proof of the superiority of humans over other beasts is that we make love when we feel moved to do so, not only for purposes of procreation. The dolphins have far outdone us on this one, and joyfully make love with whomever evokes sensuous feelings at any time. Some observers have noted what seems to be a dolphin system of hierarchy in "who may approach whom" sexually, especially within a group of captive colphins. On the other hand, one observer has seen in the open ocean a young male dolphin copulate with several females of another dolphin species, even though the males of their own herd were in full view. No one seemed to object.

No doubt Hazel's observation was correct on the day fifteen dolphins visited, when she wondered if they were mating as they rolled over one another. It seems highly probable that they were engaging in sexual intercouse,

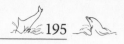
although it was not mating season, and probably the females were not in estrus and no calves would result.

But aren't dolphins monogamous? Some people feel shocked to think that the virtuous dolphin would not fulfill our ideal of keeping a lifetime mate. There really is little information about the social organization of dolphins, because there has been so little opportunity to observe them in their natural state over any extended period of time. We know that dolphins engage in sex *play* in a most uninhibited way. When it comes to *mating* for reproduction, it may be that they stay with the same partner. No one knows for certain. Or at least, the female might stay with one male. There seems to be some indications that a powerful male might have a harem of several females under his protection. My own feeling is that it is not very important. I suspect that the whole human concept of monogamy has come about through the need of human males to keep control of property (including women and children as property) that might otherwise slip out of their fingers.

We do know that dolphins form strong bonds of affection, for other dolphins, for humans, and for other ani-

mals. There are many well-documented stories of captive
dolphins who show strong attachments for other individuals over long periods of time, as well as some observations of this type of behavior among wild dolphins. We
have seen at Monkey Mia how Holey-fin and Crooked-fin,
the two mother dolphins, bring their children every day to
the beach to play, where they hobnob together much as
two human mothers would, and that these two dolphins
have been close friends for at least five years. The other
mother, Beautiful, is also close to them, but no longer
comes every day, and she and her now-grown calf seem to
have formed some attachments elsewhere, but are still
good friends with their old pals. The adolescents, Nick and
Puck are inseparable buddies, and play and fish together
almost constantly, having grown up together.

There seems to be a good deal of evidence that relationships among dolphins are matters of great importance
to them. It is rare to see a dolphin alone. In captivity
dolphins form strong attachments to other dolphins sharing their pens, even if they are of different species, and
there are poignant stories of them giving aid to one
another when ill, or of one dolphin mourning the death of
another, even preventing a dead body being removed from
the tank for a day or two.

At this time I read Frank Robson's book, *Thinking
Dolphins, Talking Whales,* which was a pure delight, and I
was so sorry I had not known of it before I went to Napier
in New Zealand. In this book he tells of the first training of
dolphins at the Marineland there, without using whistles
or rewards of fish, but by making very strong and detailed
mental images of what they wished the dolphins to do.
This method of mental communication was used with
great success for some years. But now Robson is no longer
there, and whistles and fish are used in the conventional
way by the new trainers. I would have been most interested to ask them why they changed. And how I would
have enjoyed meeting Frank Robson!

I re-read Carl Sagan's book, *The Cosmic Connection.*

especially where he tells of his meeting with a dolphin in a pool, and how the dolphin succeeded in communicating what he wanted Sagan to do (and how he maneuvered Sagan into doing it!) — and ponders how we might well practice learning to communicate with cetaceans if we are ever to communicate with any intelligance beyond our own. There is much interest in the prospect of communicating with "extra-terrestrial" beings, which we think of as out there "beyond earth." But "extra-terrestrial" means "beyond land," and extra-terrestrial intelligence could be within the waters of our own planet.

At this time, Sagan's marvelous television series, _Cosmos_ was being aired on Sunday nights, and I made a point of finding a friend who had a color television when Sunday evenings came around. I was most impressed with his moving plea for humans to take more care in their use of the earth, in order that it, and we, and all our fellow creatures may survive in good health and happiness to enjoy many more thousands of years of evolving and learning about our cosmos.

Also I read John Lilly's book, _The Mind of the Dolphin_, sequel to _Man and Dolphin_ which I had read years ago, both about communications experiments with dolphins in the Virgin Islands in the 1960s. In this second book, the research worker, Margaret Howe, tells of her two-month experiment of living as roommates in a flooded room with a young male dolphin, and how they learned to trust one another, a very touching story as well as of considerable scientific interest.

Lilly says the dolphins liked to be rewarded with stroking as much as being fed fish. But after a certain amount of stroking, they would become irritable and required _not_ being touched for a time, which I had noticed also with our dolphins.

A note I read about Dr. Lilly's new Project Janus said that he has designed a computer apparatus that will take the dolphins' high-frequency sounds, most of which are out of the range possible for us to hear, and slow them down for us humans, then take our low-pitched vocalizations and speed them up for the dolphins. The apparatus includes a video monitor as well, so that the sounds can be seen as well as heard. Hopefully in time we can all get some understanding of each others' communications.

Some weeks later on a rainy wintry morning I went to the site of Project Janus to show my slides to John and Toni Lilly. Their staff workers greeted me cordially, and while we waited for the Lillys to finish another discussion, I had a chance to visit the two young dolphins, Rosalie and Joe. I had wondered how it would be to visit captive dolphins . . . how different would they seem? I stood in a chilling drizzle, at the edge of their pool and dangled my hand in the water as I would have done at Monkey Mia, and called, "Hello Rosalie, hello Joe." They swished around in the center of the pool, ducking deep and rising again. My friend, Dean, who was with me was trying especially to get a photograph of a dolphin's eye, but it was not happening. Joe stayed submerged, turned away from us, and Rosalie was keeping her eyes closed even when she swam around on the surface, navigating with her sonar. Even when she played with the ball floating there, she opened only an occasional slit of an eye. I am told that dolphins do not use echo-location in the air, but only in water though I am not quite convinced, as bats use it very successfully in the air). Here at Project Janus, the humans usually enter the water in wet suits to relate to the dolphins, so Rosalie does not usually need to use her eyes to "see" the humans. The Monkey Mia dolphins relate to us when only our feet are in the water, so they are accustomed to using their eyes more.

Rosalie took the ball in her mouth, then with a deft movement tucked it under her body as she swam forward and then held it under one flipper, the way a football player does when going for a touchdown. She let it slip out, and it shot up out of the water diagonally to plop down near me. I picked it up and tossed it toward her. She caught it in her mouth, tucked it under and swam around, then loosed it

again in my direction. This was fun! What excellent skill she had in aiming the ball toward me! Joe ignored us completely. I was pleased that Rosalie shared her ball game with me. But I would have liked to touch her.

It was time to go meet the Lillys. Toni Lilly was very warm and welcoming, eager to see and hear of these unusual dolphins. A dozen people crowded into the tiny space and we turned on the projector. There were Crooked-fin and Nick. Holey-fin suckling baby Joy. Small children feeding fish to dolphins at their feet. Nick and Puck doing roll-overs. A view of the whole camp scene with seven people standing in the water and five dolphins being petted. Everyone was happily impressed with this remarkable phenomenon. At the end I asked if there were any questions. Dr. Lilly said, "Yes, just one. How long does it take to get there?!" Everyone wanted to go. But they concluded that they do not have time, and were off to keep up with their busy schedule. Toni Lilly gave me a hug and urged me to come again, when the staff could discuss with me any questions I might have. I will go back when the weather is warmer. I want to get in and swim with those dolphins. I look forward to asking many questions about Project Janus from John Kert, the man in charge of the research project, who also warmly urged me to return. I left feeling much drawn to this fine group of people engaged in a fascinating project.

I urge my readers to contact some of these organizations and to read some of these other books, to learn more about dolphins and to help build the chain of human understanding that will protect our friends in the waters. But meanwhile I would like to share a few amazing bits of information I have absorbed about the qualities of dolphin body and mind, to help us understand what is happening at Monkey Mia.

8

Dolphin Giftedness

One characteristic of dolphins is that they can swim very fast. When experts in hydrodynamics studied this they said that, from what they knew about shapes moving through water under a given amount of power, it was *not possible* for the dolphin to do what it is doing! I like that. It intrigues my intelligence.

It seems a British scientist named Gray discovered that, for the speed that dolphins move, they would have to have *seven times* more power than they actually do have. This became know in 1936 as Gray's Paradox. I am happy to tell you that scientists now have come to an explanation that satisfies them of how the dolphin does the impossible (so it is no longer impossible, more's the pity).

Because men would like to be able to build ships that move impossibly fast, much research was spent on trying to understand how the dolphin did it. It was learned that at least one species of dolphin (*Stenella attenuata*) can develop two-and-one-half times more muscle power output than a trained human athlete, which explains some of the difficulty, but does not solve the paradox. Normal water turbulence should still have caused more drag than it does on the dolphin's body.

A few years later another team of researchers built a hinged model of a dolphin and discovered that the powerful upward stroke of the dolphin's horizontal tail moved water past the perfectly shaped body in ways that studies of rigid models of dolphins had not revealed (you'd think that might have occurred to someone earlier). Also it had been thought that the downward stroke of the tail was the power stroke until someone observed the dolphin more carefully and found it was the upward stroke, which changed their understanding of how water flowed past the body. Even so, they figured the dolphin should not be able to swim more than about 10 knots, but was found to be able to make 15, and in some species even 22 knots.

At last in the 1970s, Gray's Paradox was laid to rest through a better understanding of the dolphin's skin. It seems there are three different characteristics of the skin that contribute to the ability of the dolphin to swim through the water at such great speed. First the skin surface has a somewhat porous, spongy quality which absorbs some water, so that there are water molecules right among the skin cells as the dolphin moves through the water. The effect is to reduce friction, as if water were moving through water. (This slight sponginess gives the skin that unusual texture when we touch it that caused little Kim to say, "It feels like wet velvet.") Second, the dolphin is actually shedding minute particles of skin as it moves through the water. The dolphin has so well adapted its body to its environment that even its skin is constantly producing tiny cells to leave behind as it swims, allowing it to slip through the water almost without touching it, so to speak. (Could this be the reason our dolphins get irritable with too much stroking, even though they love it at first? Perhaps we rub off too much skin.) Finally, the skin of the dolphin is flexible, so that as it speeds up in swimming the skin changes shape slightly, to conform to the most efficient hydrodynamic design for whatever speed it is going. So these three characteristics of the skin explain the final mysteries of how the dolphin is able to overcome the expected amount of drag, and to move so fast through the water.

The many studies of this problem over a period of forty years brought considerable respect among scientists

for the marvelous evolution of cetaceans, and caused one learned man to comment that the dolphin family is the most finely adapted group of animals in the world to their natural environment. It occurred to me that while man "adapts" his surroundings to his own wishes, the dolphin has adapted *himself* to his environment, and has produced a model of grace and joy.

The dolphin took plenty of time to do it, perhaps 40,000,000 years. *We* "do not have time." We have hands with which to make all the changes in the environment that we want, so we just make them.

Slow down, man.

Another subject of discussion about cetaceans is the question of evolution. There is much talk of the cetaceans' "return to the sea" after having been land animals. Modern dolphins still have finger bones inside their flippers and vestigial pelvic bones, so it seems they once had four limbs, used to move about. It is interesting that no old bones are found to show us what the early predecessor of the cetacean was like. But by 30,000,000 years ago there were cetacean ancestors very nearly as they are now. In the intervening eons they have had plenty of time for elegant refinements.

And elegant they are. These matters of the hydrodynamics of the dolphin body, the shape and movement of the tail, the power of the muscles, the special adaptation of the skin, all these are only a taste of the marvels of the dolphin body. For example, the regulation of heat and cold is accomplished efficiently not only by layers of blubber, but also by means of ingeniously designed blood vessels, so that the cetacean moving from arctic to tropical waters can turn up the heat or cool off at will. Unlike the cardiovascular system of any other mammal, the cetacean's blood circulation can be re-routed depending on whether the animal is feeling hot or cold. In chilly waters, veinous blood returning from the skin surface to the heart is warmed by flowing through veins that spiral around the hot-blooded arteries, so that the body interior will not be chilled by this returning blood. When the animal is swimming in tropical waters, on the other hand, the now warm veinous blood returns by a different route, to allow for heat loss and cooling.

Our human bodies are also miracles of nature, but we have surrounded ourselves with so many of the inventions of our brains and hands that our bodies are no longer so well adapted to surviving in the natural environment. We turn the electric blanket up or down instead.

Which brings us to the next big subject of discussion about dolphins: the question of their brains. There is much literature about the size and complexity of the cetacean brain, and what that may or may not mean about their intelligance. An adult human brain weighs around 1,500 grams, and we have long used this fact as one of the scientific indicators that we are more intelligent than other creatures. There is also the fact of the convolutions of the cortex, or outermost layer of the human brain, where more complicated thinking is said to be located. And a number of other factors.

It happens that the brain of the bottlenosed dolphin weighs around 1,800 grams, or 300 grams more than the human one, and has at least as many convolutions of the cerebral cortex! We may say, "But the dolphin has a bigger body, so of course it has a bigger brain." It doesn't work that way. Horses and cows have big bodies, but not big brains. It is true that the bottlenosed dolphin is somewhat larger than a man, but an enormous tiger shark, which lives in the same environment as the dolphin, has a brain weighing only *100* grams! Not much of the large dolphin brain is actually used to regulate and maneuver the body. It occurs to me that possibly the sperm whale evolved such a huge body simply in order to *contain and move around* its incredibly enormous brain, which is *five times* the size of ours.

What do the dolphins use their great brains for? We know that we use our big brains for such things as language, processing abstract thought, and to manipulate our marvelous hands to make all the fabulous *things* we create. The dolphin has no hands, and no possessions. That alone seems to us to limit enormously what the dolphin might be doing with its brain. Our brain is much occupied with manipulating our hands, and even our thoughts and our speech, are much occupied with thinking and talking about our things — how we invent them, make them, buy them and use them, and how to keep them in good condition, how to repair them, even how to get rid of them. Try to *imagine* going through a day without thinking or talking about any possessions. Or better yet, try to *go* through a day that way!

What in the world could the dolphin be using its brain for? There has been some study of this question, and we know a few answers, but much more is to be learned. For one thing, the dolphin brain is much engaged in processing sensory perceptions, as is ours. A very large part of our brain is used to process and interpret our visual perceptions, while some other animals are more concentrated on their sense of smell. The dolphin apparently has no sense of smell at all, but has very good eyesight. The dolphin's primary sense, however, is the sense of hearing, and much of its brain is involved in processing those perceptions. Not only does the dolphin hear acutely all the sounds in its environment — sounds of the sea's motion and sounds of other creatures of the sea (including fish it must catch to eat), sounds made by other dolphins, and sounds that humans are adding to the underwater world — besides all this symphony of sound coming to the dolphin from other sources, there are the sounds that the dolphin is making for itself. It sends out sounds that bounce off the sea bottom and off rocks to tell it where it is, that bounce off fish that it catches to eat, that bounce off other dolphins so it knows where its friends and relations are, and that bounce off us when we are there. All these sounds return to the dolphin and are processed to give it millions of bits of information, not only about the location of all these objects, but about textures and conditions and qualities. A

picture comes to my mind of a woman fingering a piece of
cloth, examining the texture and rejecting or approving its
quality based on her experienced perception. Her brain
receives impulses from her fingers and eyes, and processes
those impressions relative to the memories of many similar experiences stored in the brain. The dolphin can do this
sort of examination with its echo-location sounds that it
sends out to bounce back and be processed by its brain,
without necessarily using its senses of sight or touch. It
does also use its eyes and touch. The dolphin has a very
highly developed tactile sense, so that the brain processes
in detail all the delicate nuances of information about
what the dolphin touches.

This gives us a picture of dolphin life having a very
strong sense of place. The dolphin is also a very mobile
creature, constantly moving, moving, moving, and is
therefore constantly changing its reading on location and
position.

When I travel all the time, I don't *do* as much. Consciousness is occupied with locating myself, feeling the
energy of the places I am traveling through and of the
people involved, and adjusting my energy to it. I'm involved in *being* in those places and in that movement, as
in walking on a beach or forest trail. One reason it is so
pleasant to be in nature is because we get out of the
thoughts that we go round and round in most of the time
in our heads. Instead, we get into perceiving all the sights
and sounds and scents and temperatures.

A dolphin's life is much occupied with perceiving. It is
a moving creature, constantly taking readings on where
everything is, and what the textures and qualities are.

It is very pleasant for me to close my eyes and imagine
how it would be to live in a world where my whole being
senses its relatedness to everything else. The sense of heat
and cold never giving discomfort because of my own ability to adapt to it; the sense of weightlessness in the water,
moving up and down in the third dimension as readily as
in the surface plane, always fluid and flowing; the aware-

ness of the masses of big boulders and sea floor and the lighter masses of coral formations and kelp, the twinkling masses of schools of fish, and the darting or crawling movements of single sea creatures; the slow rhythms of the sea itself in its currents and tides, overlaid by the dancing palpitations of the waves and wavelets on top; and the warm, cuddling, racing, exciting, reassuring presence of one's fellow dolphins, close and nudging, near and resting, far and gliding, approaching and leaping, receding and following. So the dolphin's brain is much occupied with its life of location, constantly relating, relating, moving and relating, positioning, touching, drifting, relating.

The dolphins also make other sounds, such as the ones Nick and Puck and B.B. used to make at Monkey Mia when they would say "Ooo Ooo Ooo." There are volumes of literature on the question of whether the different whistles and squeaks and creaking noises that dolphins make are "language" in the human sense. Opinions seem to vary hugely. One view is that it might be possible to break the sounds down into syllables and phrases (as we use language) that could then tell us stories of life in the sea. The opposite view sees whistles and squeaks as no more than grunts and chortles, perhaps expressive of emotion.

My own feeling when reading all these discussions, and based on my personal relationship with dolphins, is that we get a little lost in our own experiences of both intellect and emotion. My intuition is that dolphins are neither as intellectual (different from intelligent, mind you) nor as emotional as we humans, or at least that their consciousness is not as preoccupied with intellect and emotion as ours tends to be. I would guess that dolphins most definitely do communicate very precisely with one another (and "at" us, although our reception is not very clear), but probably not in anything remotely like our syllable-and-phrase language.

I feel that dolphin "knowingness" is very holistic. The fact that much of their sensory perception is involved in spatial reationships seems to support this. We know that

in our own brains the side of the brain that has understanding of spatial relationships (the right side in most of us) is
also where intuition, or "whole knowing" seems to be
located . . . where we know something at once, rather than
step by step as in sequential reasoning. Language, on the
other hand, is located on the other (left) side of our brains,
where we can understand something *only* sequentially,
step by step. My intuition tells me (right brain!) that the
dolphins are very holistically oriented. I wonder if they
possess anything at all like our sequential reasoning, that
we are so obsessed with in our culture? Or anything like
our language? Most of the old cultures of the world had a
far greater orientation towards intuitive (holisitc or
"wholistic") knowing before the European culture spread
over the earth and conquered it all with its left-brain
technology. Now many of us who have experienced the
highest educational, cultural and technical advantages
our society can offer, are seeking to re-awaken the ancient
intuitive knowledge that brings us more into balance and
harmony with the earth and one another.

After all the study of the dolphin brain, I do not feel
that we have even a remote understanding of what the
dolphin is using its large brain for. Scientists go on to
speculate about the "intelligence" of the dolphin with its
big and complex brain, and many comment that since we
have great difficulty defining and even more in testing
"intelligence" in our own species, it is a bit presumptuous
of us to judge the intelligence of another large-brained
species.

But humans are nothing if not presumptuous. So we
dissect the brain of our brother the dolphin, watch him
sort out dimes from pennies in a muddy sea floor, make
recordings of his sounds to analyze on our fancy machines,
and stroke our chins and say, "Yes, I do believe the fellow is
intelligent."

One can imagine the dolphins looking at our big
brains with their in-depth sonar vision, and then observe
us discarding radio-active wastes into the sea, killing each

other *en masse* in wars, and eating ourselves sick just to satisfy our tongue-and-mouth cravings. Then the dolphins might process this information in their built-in computers, and signal to each other, "They have a very large and complex brain, compared to our friends the fishes. But they do strangely stupid things."

9

Is There A Message?

Let us return to the question of whether the dolphins have a message for us. As I have said elsewhere in these pages, my attempts to "contact" them in meditation did not result in any words, in the manner of Moses on the mountain. My intuitive feeling is that there is not a message in the sense of, "Go and tell the humans that ... (whatever) ... "

On the other hand, there is a clear and simple message in their very presence there at our feet, and that is: "Let's be friends. Let's get to know each other."

As I said to Wilf and Hazel towards the end of my stay in 1980, it seems quite possible that this pod of dolphins simply live there in that particular part of Shark Bay, and Hazel and Wilf and the fishing camp people simply live there on that beach. The dolphins are curious to see what their neighbors do from day to day, and come to share a friendly touch from time to time, and the humans are curious to see what the dolphins do, and also like to share touch now and then. There is a herd of some 100 dugongs that live a few miles farther out the Peron Peninsula, and I can well imagine another pod of dolphins going there frequently to watch what their neighbors the dugongs are doing, and give them a friendly nudge or two, if that is welcomed by dugongs. Surely one of the main reasons the dolphins continue to visit is that their overtures are met with enthusiasm on the part of the humans. But the enthusiasm is not overdone.

It is interesting to me to see that the people who live at Monkey Mia and the fishing families who come there for regular long stays are not very... well... obsessed with the dolphins. They are interested in them. They love them. They are concerned for their safety and well-being. They enjoy them. But they do not go into raptures of sentimentality or mysticism over their contact with dolphins. Perhaps it is partly a trait of the Australian character, which is generally rather matter-of-fact and no-nonense, yet deeply good-hearted and caring. Their attitude towards the dolphins is very much as it would be towards some rather unusual human neighbors.

This attitude fits quite will with the dolphins' approach, as they also have no trace of sentimentality or mysticism that is discernable to the objective observer. One of the deeply stirring qualities of the experience of being with the dolphins is that feeling of being stripped of all pretense and hypocrisy. The dolphin is just right there with us. When the dolphin looks at us, we have a profound feeling of being exposed, that the dolphin sees us for exactly what we are. At first it is a little disconcerting. Then we realize that the dolphin accepts what it sees. And that is a fine feeling. It reminds me of the old saying: "A friend is someone who knows all about you and likes you anyway." Perhaps acceptance of one another as we are is a message from the dolphins.

If it is by example that the dolphins bring their messages, then surely there are several fine lessons we might learn. Lessons of grace, freedom, joy. Ah, freedom. How can we become more free? Americans and Europeans are spending millions every year on medication, psychiatric counseling, and various sorts of therapeutic training to try to free themselves of tensions. Behold the dolphin!

Several times in these pages I have spoken of the

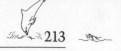

message of simplicity that seems to be given by the dolphins, the lesson that we do not need all these possessions to be happy. Of course we are not going to return to the life of Adam and Eve, and would not be able to survive the first storm if we gave up our clothing and shelter. But many of us have already learned that a plethora of possessions can be a terrible hindrance to a free and joyful life. The acquisition, maintenance and guarding of land, house, furnishings, clothing, jewelry, works of art, vehicles, hobby and sports paraphernalia, etc. *ad nauseam*, consume awesome amounts of time and energy. Many of us, after spending years urgently acquiring more and more possessions, have found later that life is more pleasurable when we simplify the number and complexity of our possessions, at least to some degree. We gain some freedom, and space to evolve in new ways.

It has occurred to me often in my travels about the world that our intelligence is missing an essential ingredient. Our intellect has enabled us to create a marvelous technology, and to produce a host of magnificent art forms, from architecture to music and literature. But our intellect is lacking in both personal and collective wisdom. In an article I wrote some years ago about orangutans, I spoke of "man's foolish intelligence," because we seem to have such poor judgement in applying our intelligence to the world's problems. We often seem to be just making things worse!

In *The Ascent of Man*, Branowski comments movingly on the pleasure we humans experience in developing our skills. We love to learn a new skill, and then to be able to do it better and better, and then beyond what anyone has ever done before. This striving for excellence brings great satisfaction.

There are some marvelous music programs on the public television station, and I enjoy watching them even more than in a concert hall because the television camera can show us very close views of the performers. One evening I was watching a requiem, with two men and two

women soloists and a large choir and orchestra. The
music was superb, and I was spellbound to see the intimate views of the faces of the performers and the conductor as they poured their souls into the fountain of music
they were all creating together. I thought what a privilege
it is to be one of those human beings, engaged in a group
work of such transcendent beauty, how deeply satisfying,
not only to all of them, but to many thousands of us
watching and listening. After the long performance an
interviewer spoke with the conductor and two of the soloists. It was very touching to see them, quite tired, but also
deeply moved, as they spoke quietly and simply of their
experience in the performance. It was as if the intensity of
the music had somehow purified them, leaving them in a
very whole and complete state of grace.

On another evening I watched the transmissions from
the spacecraft Voyager II as it passed through the rings of
Saturn. Since I was a small child and had my first glimpse
through a backyard telescope of this strange planet with
its surrounding rings, I had been fascinated to know more
about it. Now here were pictures of how it all looks at
close range, even passing among the many rings . . . beautiful to see. It was exciting, too, to hear the reports of the
information transmitted to the laboratory here on earth,
and to learn that much was different from what the scientists had expected to find. But most interesting of all to me
was to see the faces of these scientists as they were interviewed one by one. They had been watching the transmissions for 24 hours, intent upon the information received
from the spacecraft, hours that formed the peak of their
professional lives. How marvellously exciting it must
have been for them! All their understanding of this part of
our solar system was being confirmed or enlarged upon,
bit by bit. I have almost no training in this field, so I
understood little intellectually, but it was easy to share
their experience of a profound opening of knowledge. Like
the music performers, they were very tired, but deeply
moved and fulfilled, and again I had that impression of

them being somehow purified . . . all dross burned away in the fire of an intense experience.

Some years ago I watched the Olympic Games when they were telecast from Munich. I have very little interest in sports games, but found myself entranced to see these beautiful displays of human physical perfection. The television camera gave us wonderful close views of athletes, showing the grace and coordination and power of the finely developed bodies as they performed with the most elegant precision. It also showed us the emotion of the faces, whether expressing quiet satisfaction or jubilant rejoicing in skills magnificently perfected.

These are portraits of human beings at our best, and how wonderful we are at such times! Using our intelligence, our intuition, our emotional power, our skills and discipline, working together, sharing it all with a great mass of other humans . . . how profoundly *good* we are then!

Never would I suggest that we should not engage in activites that bring us so much joy and satisfaction. Can we still derive this great pleasure in our skills without pressing upon nature so destructively? The dolphin clearly gets much pleasure from its bodily sensations, from skill and precision and power, from coordinating with its fellows, perhaps from using its great brain. But it destroys nothing except the fish it eats. Can we learn something from this? Can we enjoy using our intellect and body skills without making such disruptive changes in our natural surroundings?

We humans just *have* to study things, to satisfy our thirst for learning, understanding, knowledge. Can we study the dolphins, without interfering with them? At Monkey Mia there is an opportunity to observe them regularly. Can we do that without disrupting their lives? Could we let them be the leaders of mutual study between us, letting them learn about us as we learn about them? We must refrain from imbedding radio transmitting devices in order to follow them. Imagine how horrible that would be for a creature who uses sounds to perceive his surroundings; to have a foreign device creating static among his own sounds.

We humans, especially we European-origin humans, enormously value our intellect and our intellectual achievements. The question argued about dolphins — "how intelligent are they?" — really means, "How much are they to be valued?" If they are very "intelligent," then they are of more value. One of the most effective arguments against even the accidental killing of dolphins is that they are so intelligent, "like us." Perhaps they are of more value because they have learned to live so happily and so non-destructively. Is that not a sign of the greatest intelligence?

One measure we use to judge intelligence in other animals is whether they can learn to use a tool. What this really does is reveal *what it is that we regard as of value.* Because we evolved our brain and hands together, and learned to use tools and to make all these amazing technological marvels, we believe that the first trace of such an ability in another creature would indicate something of value, something to be admired. We regard our hands as the biological development which, coupled with our brains, made it possible for us to become "superior." Because our hands are able to *do* the things that our intellect divises, we have been able to "conquer" the earth and all its creatures. We regard an animal as being of superior intelligence if it learns to use a "tool" to manipulate its environment in some way.

But is it "smart" to manipulate the environment to the point of destruction? Is it not perhaps an intelligence to be questioned that leads us to the brink of disaster in the name of progress? Is it possible that some of the other creatures, who do not indulge in manipulation as we do may have found a way to enjoy their intelligence with more wisdom than we?

We are not going to give up using and enjoying our skills, but perhaps the key is to become more aware, more

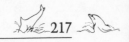

conscious, more mindful moment by moment of how the things we do affect the overall harmony of nature.

What have we done with our technological marvels? We have made lives for ourselves that cut us off from nature, and that are rapidly changing this old earth itself to the point that parts of it are becoming untenable for all the other (less intelligent?) creatures, as well as for ourselves. Let us pursue these two themes for a bit: first, the extent to which we have cut ourselves off from nature, and second, the familiar charge that we are ruining the environment, altering the habitat so that it no longer nourishes the creatures who evolved to fit that habitat.

When I came back to live in cities after several years of travel in more natural areas, I was impressed with the extent to which our daily lives are out of touch with nature. We have almost no physical touch with any natural surroundings. The buildings we live in are built of materials that have been processed almost beyond recognition of their origin, as is the stuff of which our clothing is made. The articles in our rooms are almost all the products of our hands and machines. We may enter our traveling machine from within our house, but even if we step outside to reach it, we do so on a concrete pavement, and after riding to our destination we enter another artificial environment. The very air inside these spaces is artificially heated, cooled and filtered. Many of the city dwellers I know cannot tell me what direction their bedroom window faces, whether north, south, east or west. "When does the sun come to your window?" "I never noticed. I guess I have the drapes drawn most of the time." These people are living in caves. Building codes require a certain amount of window area per floor space, but when windows are permanently locked and drapes kept drawn, walls may as well be windowless. Offices and factories and large stores shelter workers who have no way to glimpse the sky during their long day, and cannot tell of it is daylight or dark, if it is raining or snowing or sparkling sun.

Even when we venture out into our gardens we are in a world created by man, for the plants there, the trees, shrubs, grass and flowers, are almost without exception hybridized by man. When we go into the countryside, the pastures and fields, whether planted with grain or crops, orchards or vineyards, all are again plants that have been tampered with by man. Even where there are bits of forest, often the trees growing there are not native to that region. If they have not been planted there purposefully by man, they may have sprung from seed drifted there from some man-planted growth nearby. The very air is filled with tiny particles of man-produced pollutants.

Ah, there are the birds. They are our one touch with nature in our garden. But even many of the birds are species that are not natural to the area where we live, but have been brought from another land by some homesick early settlers. We must go to the high mountains or the seashore or some special reserve to seek direct contact with our planet earth in its *natural* state. And there we are likely to find some cans and bottles and plastic wrappers, or some photographic film container, to make sure we know that our fellow human has been there before us. And we are wearing our nylon windbreaker and our composition boots, or if the weather is hot, we may be wearing our fashionable swim togs and our suntan lotion.

"What of it?" you may ask. "If we have changed our environment so much from its original form, does it matter? We have made it more comfortable and convenient."

It seems to me there are two ways in which this is not so much to be admired. First, we may question how good it is for us. Then surely we must question what we are doing to the other creatures of our earth. Not only have we changed our environment, but we (and all other inhabitants of our earth) are much changed by our modifications.

For ourselves, there is a change that comes in us whether we are in touch with the natural conditions of our earth or are encapsulated in our protective cocoon. Any of us can find a deep refreshment of spirit by going for a walk

in the forest or the seashore, if we turn our consciousness *out of our intellectual and emotional ruminations* and tune in to sensing the world around us. Almost without exception we find this an inspiriting event, to be in touch with nature. If we turn our attention to observing, and our consciousness to being aware of the sights and sounds and scents of nature we find our tensions falling away, our depressions flooded over with renewed hope, and our sense of awkwardness in our daily trials replaced with a sense of grace.

My good friend Dean Campbell, who takes wondrous photographs of nature, has helped open my eyes to all the tiny details of nature's designs. The miraculous intricacy of the minute parts and the glory of their perfect relationships is revealed in every leaf and bud and flower, in every sunbeam and cloud and dewdrop. Is there any one among us who does not feel a falling away of weight on the spirit when we allow ouselves to notice these miracles? They are always there around us. Take a moment to look around you.

When I first began my six years of world travel, I had just read Lyall Watson's book, *Super Nature,* which opened my awareness to how "super" our natural world is, how related, how harmonious its rhythms. In my travels I have discovered a whole new dimension for enjoying life, simply by allowing myself to experience more of the natural world. By living outdoors a great deal more, and in places that have not been so changed from their natural state by the hand of man, I have discovered responses within myself that I had not known were there. I have become so much more aware of the hour of sunset and sunrise at different seasons and at different latitudes. There is a special vibration of life at those times of day that I had not realized before. Now I always like to be awake at dawn to feel that magic change that comes as the light creeps over the earth. I have become aware of the feel of the phases of the moon, and at any given time I know what shape of moon I will see and at what hour of the night or day. I am

aware of bird migrations, and their times of mating plum-
age, of the sprouting, flowering and fruiting times of
plants.

I believe that other creatures of the earth *always
know this*, and that the rhythms of these things do affect
our human bodies and spirits at some level of our being. It
is a profoundly good feeling, a sense of healing, to become
aware of these cosmic rhythms.

Becoming more aware of how we are affected *by* nature would result, I believe, in realizing how we affect our
natural world by the things we do. And we would care
more. In small ways we would alter our daily behavior to
be less destructive to the earth.

One of the first things I had to cope with when I began
world traveling was the realization that it is not really
important to be comfortable. I had lived a fairly typical
upper-middle-class American life, with instant hot water,
a heated and cooled house and office, a soft bed and chairs,
a roomy automobile. I was quite addicted to bodily com-
fort, living in my padded cocoon, in rhythm with a clock
and appointment calendar rather than with the sun and
seasons. Later, when I rode on a bus through the
Himalayas in India, jammed with five persons on a hard
seat that we would think is not really wide enough for two,
in the steaming heat, for fourteen hours . . . I was absolutely astounded to find that I could arrive at my destination in a state of bliss. How was that possible? Because I
had learned by that time that it is of no importance if my
body is comfortable or not. On a limited budget, it is the
only way that it is possible to see the imcomparable
Himalayas, and I was not going to miss it because it was
not comfortable.

We look out the window on an icy day and we see the
little birds, and we think how cold their little feet must be
clasping the frosty branches. Then on a summer day when
the thermometer reaches over a hundred, again we see the
little birds, hopping about on the hot pavement. Their
little feet must be burning. But they do get along through

these extremes of seasons. As did humans until not so long ago. Now we have lived for only two or three genera- tion is buildings that are kept artificially cooled as well as heated, and what has happened to us? We have a tolerance of not more than about four degrees one way or another from our favorite temperature. When there is more varia- tion than that, we actually suffer. *Is it possible that it can be healthy for the future of our species to be able to adapt so little?*

One of the most interesting books I have read in a long while is *The Timeless Land*, by Eleanor Dark. It is a novel, but based on historical characters and events of the ear- liest settlement of Australia by the English. It begins with the aborigines who were living there when the first sailing ships came, and tells of their reactions as they became acquainted with the strange folk who were settling in their land. It is fiction, of course, but I feel that the author has given us a very perceptive view of how it must have seemed to the aborigines. One of the things that amazed them was the clothing of these newcomers. They them- selves had never worn clothing, and had, as all other ani- mals do, adapted themselves to changes in heat and cold. Of course these absurd English wore clothing that was not even appropriate to the climate they were living in, but rather what was considered "proper" to wear back in Eng- land.

The native people were impressed with how little awareness the invaders had of the natural world around them, as for instance in the matter of food. It was clear that the people in the new colony were nearly starving, but when expeditions went out to search for food, they went right past perfectly good nourishing food, and went back empty-handed. How could they pass by these edible roots and lizards? And then the aborigines reasoned that anyone who covered his skin, so that he had no contact with the air and the sun and the earth, could not of course, be in very good communication with nature and its bounty. If you covered your skin from contact with nature, how could you know and receive what the earth had to offer you?

In many ways, then, we modern "civilized" humans have surrounded ourselves with a thicker and thicker "skin cover." Are we evolving into creatures who have less and less ability to adapt to even the usual rhythms of change in nature, much less to the havoc of storms and earthquakes?

What of the slow but drastic changes we are bringing about on the earth? What of the "desertification" effects of human actions? We cut and burn huge areas of forests and plow or pave over great areas of earth. We pour strange substances into the water, and bring together unstudied mixtures of plants and insects.

When Europeans first came to America, there were other humans here who, as in the case of the Australian aborigines, had a much more harmonious relationship to the natural environment around them. One of my favorite stories of the native American tribes (most of them are too heartbreaking for me to read!) is the story of Ishi. The book, *Ishi, Last of His Tribe,* by Theodora Kroeber, is the true account of how the last few individuals of this particular tribe lived together beside a small stream in the forest for year after year. Although there were people of the new civilization very nearby, no one ever discovered Ishi's people living there. They went through season after season, harvesting acorns and drying them, making baskets to store them in, catching fish and rabbits, telling the old stroies to their young, taking care of the dying aged, and no one knew they were there. How was it possible for them to remain undiscovered? It was because they made so little impact on the earth where they lived. When they harvested grass seed, it was not noticeable. When they fished they did not disturb the stream. Their places of dwelling were made of natural materials that were taken from the forest without leaving raw gashes. Of course in this case, these people were being especially careful not to be discovered, but it was their natural way of life to behave in such a way

as to make little change in the flow of nature around them.

All over the earth there have been humans who lived this way for thousands of years ... until the people of European origin came. It is not humans as a whole who have such a bad record of "conquering" nature wherever they went. There is something about the culture of the *Euopeans* that has made people everywhere take on a way of life that disregards the needs of all the other creatures that share our planet, and even the needs of the earth itself. The technology of the Europeans was so persuasive because of its power to destroy. We were able to conquer and subjugate the other people of the world, which made our technology seem admirable. We despised the "weak" cultures we encountered, and taught those peoples to despise their own cultures.

I remember standing on the beach at Bali one day at sunset. It is the custom there for the whole family to go to the beach at that time of day, and many foreign visitors also go to watch the sunset. The foreign tourists were mostly wearing shirts and blouses and sarongs made of the beautiful Balinese batik cotton cloth. But the local Balinese people were wearing clothing made of Occidental style synthetic material! A few years ago, every Balinese dressed in a simple loose cotton garment wrapped around his or her waist, and nothing more. It was a sensible and appropriate way to dress in that hot and humid climate. Now the men wear Occidental-style long pants made of dark synthetic cloth, which must be very hot and miserably uncomfortable, and every Balinese woman seems to have a whole wardrobe of nylon brassieres which are worn under nylon blouses. The government has posters all over the island admonishing the people to "dress decently." (In order even to understand the admonition it is necessary to develop a concept that the body is "indecent.") Balinese are taking to wearing socks and shoes of Western style, as well as long-sleeved shirts and blouses, and other items quite inappropriate for their climate and economy. What is there about Occidental style clothing that is so attractive?

It can only be that people of Western culture wear it, and
the Western culture has been able to use its technology to
conquer the world, so all Western customs therefore, must
be superior.

Throughout the world, many charming houses of
bamboo and coconut palm combined with earthen bricks
and handsomely carved wood, which used to have hand-
woven mats on the floor to sit or lie on, now have tin roofs
that make them into ovens, and are crowded with furni-
ture of Occidental style, including stuffed mattresses
which are so much hotter than the simple and organic
woven mats.

It is said that half of the world's nations are starving
while the others diet. Our efforts to help the starving lead
us to patronize them and teach them to despise their old
ways. Our technology is so impressive that they accept
what we teach in this regard, and long for our consumer
goods. But if all humans lived with our level of goods the
earth would be consumed in a short time. It may even do
so with only less than half the world consuming at the
level of America and Europe.

Is it possible for us to learn to be satisfied, contented,
happy with fewer possesions? With less indulgence?

We need to develop some appreciation of the sensitiv-
ity of these old cultures in their relation to environment
and to the rhythms of nature. We assume those people are
suffering because they have so much "less" than we have.
We see neither *their* strength in their simplicity, nor our
own very real suffering in our plenty.

Some of our attitudes are beginning to change. We are
learning more respect for cultures we once despised, learning to admire their deeper understanding of nature's har-
monies. It is not too late for us to modify our lives to have
more awareness of the earth's needs and those of all her
other creatures. The dolphins are a good place to begin.
They are so quick to understand and encourage us.

The problem with human impact on the earth is not
so much over-population as it is the destructive way we

over-use the earth's resources. We overeat, use too many clothes, build too much shelter space, create too many toys and gadgets using too much energy. American cars are much larger than they need to be, and use too much metal, too much gasoline, and require too much of the earth to be paved . . . and on and on.

What is needed is for *each* human being to learn to live more harmoniously with nature. Each of us must learn not to consume so much. We don't need it, and it doesn't even give us satisfaction to be so extravagant. Those of us who have tried it *enjoy* living a simpler life with a more daily, hourly awareness of nature. "What would be the natural way to do it?" would be a good guide for daily life.

From this more natural perspective we can meet our dolphin friends, and perhaps many others. Imagine a day when we could step outside our door and have the birds that are flying by stop to greet us . . . and squirrels and raccoons or whatever creatures ordinarily live in our surroundings. Every child has had some story book with animals who behave this way towards us. At Monkey Mia the dolphins make this story come true for many children. Perhaps some of these youngsters may be able to carry it on into their later life and experience a special relationship with other creatures . . . and even develop a similar relationship, of deep acceptance and trust, with their fellow human beings.

Dolphins have one quality that is most impressive. It may be called forgiveness. Veterinarians who attend dolphins in captivity have commented that whereas other animals of considerable intelligence, (such as chimpanzees), remember the doctor's syringe and react to his next visit with expressions of dislike and fear, dolphins do not. One veterinarian's comment was that they seem to know that our intention is to help, despite the pain. I am sure that that is true. Other examples show that they continue to give us every opportunity to be our best in our relationships with them, no matter how many times we transgress.

It seems to me that this is the embodiment of what most human religions try to teach. Love one another. Forgive those who trespass. Learn to let go whatever arises, observe and let go, as my Buddhist teacher said. Be aware of your emotions, accept them, act on them if appropriate, and then let go, as the most modern Western therapists are now saying. This the dolphin does to perfection. If it is irritated with us, it shows it immediately, and then is ready to love us again at once. Of all the messages we might learn from the dolphin's example, this is perhaps the most important.

Another subject that comes up again and again in the pages of my journal is the phenomenon of fear in humans, and how that influences our behavior, preventing us from being able to enjoy many of the opportunities for pleasure we might have. Much of our senseless cruelty and destruction to the other creatures who share our planet comes from our fear of them.

Why are we so afraid? We have not been harmed that much. When we are afraid something may hurt us, we hurt it first.

It is interesting to contrast our fearful behavior with the behavior of the trusting cetaceans. There has been much comment over the years on the fact that the great whales of yore almost never did any harm to the puny men in their cockleshell boats who came to slaughter and butcher them. They did not even flee, but in fact gathered around, and exposed themselves to their doom, as if they were more curious than anything else.

It is said that an injured whale would seem to call the others for help, and they would approach and cluster around. But it appears that in fact they did nothing to save the injured one. Perhaps they did not call "help", but only "something is happening here." They could easily have lashed their great tails and upset the little rowboats from which the men harpooned them. It seems that on the rare occasions that this did happen, it was only when the movements of the injured animal bumped into the boat by *accident.* If several of the huge creatures had come up under the sailing ship they could have overturned it and ended the entire whale hunt. Probably even one whale alone could have done this. Why did they not attack and destroy the human tormentors?* Even today, although the whaling ships are much bigger, they could do much damage. Why do they never try? Some say this is proof that cetaceans could not possibly be very intelligent.

Dolphins have never been known to kill a human even when their calves are being captured (yet their intelligence comes into play to *help* a human in distress). Cousteau in his book, *Dolphins,* tells about one of his men who was capturing dolphins. The diver had succeeded in grasping a fine big dolphin calf with his mechanical catcher. As he was appraising how perfect for his purposes this specimen would be, the mother dolphin appeared on the scene! He was frightened, expecting to attacked (as he well deserved). What did she do, this great 300 pound healthy dolphin, quite capable of ramming him and doing serious injury? She did not attack. She simply swam round and round him, making urgent sounds! (Crying and pleading, was the way he perceived it.) He felt in a terrible dilemma. A very great amount of effort and expense had gone into the Costeau team's attempt to catch a fine young animal, and now he had one in his grasp but he felt that it was too cruel to both the mother and calf to take the little one away. He found himself unable to keep his valuable catch. He let the calf free, and with its mother it quickly swam away into the deep. (Wonderful! It is difficult for me to imagine how anyone could take any dolphin into captivity.)

---

*There is one documented instance of a sperm whale charging a whaling ship head on, and sinking it. This was in the South Pacific in 1820. It is said that this incident was the basis for Herman Melville's classic novel *Moby Dick.* It is interesting that, because of the fine *literary* quality of this book, millions of students over several generations have been required to read it, and have been subjected to this ominous view of whales, when actually it was based on a most atypical occurrence.

But why did the mother not attack? It is said that dolphins have been known to kill sharks, that they gather great speed and ram the shark in exactly the right place to rupture the liver. Clearly they could do the same to a human, but have never been known to do so. Some humans feel that dolphins will protect us from sharks, and that it is therefore safe to swim where there are sharks if dolphins are also present. Shark-bite wounds are often found on dolphins, and presumably sharks do kill dolphins, though it seems only sick ones that are undefended by other dolphins. On the other hand dolphins are frequently seen to swim peacefully in the same waters with sharks, with neither molesting the other. Humans tend to react by automatically killing creatures we regard as dangerous, notably insects and reptiles, if we merely find them in our presence. We fear that they might harm us, so we protect ourselves by attacking first.

Fichtelius and Sjolander speculate in *Smarter than Man?* whether humans learned down through the ages to fight and destroy because carnivorous humans had to fight to get food, in competition with other fiercer carnivores in areas of scarce hunting. They propose that the cetaceans perhaps never had to learn to fight because their food is plentiful and easy to catch.

It has been suggested to me that whales do not attack us when we injure members of their families because they do not understand cause and effect. They do not know that we are *causing* an injury, but only that injury is happening. This is quite an interesting thought, and the explanation of *not connecting* cause and effect does fit the whales behavior when they come in response to the call of an injured one but do nothing to destroy the human molesters.

In Eastern religions one of the concepts that is considered a very deep understanding is that ultimately nothing is caused. Everything just is. This teaching results in a total acceptance of all events — "It's just what's happening" — without feeling attachment to the outcome. When one reaches this stage of understanding, events in the material world, including any extreme of pain or pleasure, are of no significance, but may be viewed with interest from a far perspective, as one enjoys watching a drama. Then one may decide how involved one wishes to be, simply as a matter of choice, as the outcome is of no significance. It could be that the cetaceans have reached this stage of highly evolved consciousness, and that might explain their behavior.

There seems to be a notable lack of fear in whales and dolphins. Caution and care are exercised with skill, but these seem to require experience and perhaps judgement without necessarily the emotion of fear. How does fear, or other emotion, come about? We humans tend to believe that fear is created by the approach of the fearsome thing — the snake creeping towards us. But actually the small child tends to be curious rather than frightened by such things, until conditioned by the mother's gasp and frantic reaction. Thereafter the emotion of fear arises in the child when a snake approaches. But it is not created by the snake. It is created by the connection made in the mind. It is caused by what we tell ourselves about snakes. A trained reptile handler, who knows the characteristics and habits of the snake and how to grasp it does not tell herself that she is in danger, and does not feel fear.

In the book *Kinship with All Life* there is a fascinating description of how a woman "gentled" snakes that were considered to be very dangerous by those who brought them to her. This book by J. Allen Boone published thirty years ago is a beautiful manual on how to establish a deep understanding of communicating with animals of various kinds, from dogs to flies, with the result of a deeply blessed feeling of oneness with all sentient beings. Much of this is accomplished through letting go of our conviction of human superiority, as well as through letting go of fear.

Again I wonder, why are humans so filled with fear? Our lives are troubled not only by fear of animals but by fear of the future, fear of ill health and death, fear of

Again I wonder, why are humans so filled with fear? Our lives are troubled not only by fear of animals but by fear of the future, fear of ill health and death, fear of humiliation, fear of failure in our strivings, fear of earthquakes, fear of loss of possessions or loss of love, fear of one another. Of all these perhaps the last is most justified, as we truly have done the most terrible things to one another. Fear is created not be the world around us, but in the mind, by what we think is *going* to happen. Perhaps the easiest of all our fears to let go of, would be our fear of the other animals on our planet. At least within the time of human history, we have dominated and protected ourselves so thoroughly from attack by animals that although our treatment of them is incredibly thoughtless or even deliberately cruel, there is very little incidence of animals attacking us, giving humans *cause* to fear them. When we do allow our fears to fall away from us, we often have marvelous experiences of sharing with our fellow creatures.

There is an article in the February 1981 issue of National Geographic that illustrates this possibility. Some scuba divers were enjoying the waters of the Gulf of California, and saw a huge manta ray, six meters across from tip to tip of its great wingspread. Imagine what an awesome sight such a huge creature would be when one is in the water with it! This manta had been injured in a fish net, and still carried trailing pieces of rope which had dug into its flesh, and there was festering of the tissues. One woman diver was moved by the sight of this suffering to try to help. She let go of her fear of the huge but slow-moving creature, and sank down through the water to rest on its back, where she pulled out the ropes from the damaged flesh. Then the great fellow slowly flapped off through the water carrying her for a ride. What a lovely experience it must have been. Later, others rode him, down into the deep and up and around. Eventually a second large ray provided a ride!

What was the key to this event? I would say it was a change of human attitude. Loss of fear. The article speaks of the animals being temporarily tamed, but I doubt the animals were so changed. These humans were behaving very differently, not running scared but actually helping an injured creature. The *feèl* of the interaction for the big ray must have been very different from the usual experience wild creatures have at our hands.

What will be the future of humans with other beings? May the future of the dolphin-human relationship at Monkey Mia be a key to this larger question? Will more and more dolphins come to the beach there, and encourage more and more contact with humans? Will this phenomenon occur in other places? With other kinds of free animals? As humans let go of fear it seems that it might happen that way. And this will surely help us if we do find, as many think we may, life in the distant spaces of our cosmos. We hope we will not automatically fear and perhaps destroy strange life forms before we can learn their nature.

10

Knowing

One person I talked with in California, a man named Joe McCord, had an experience with dolphins that is a really magical tale to tell. He had been scuba diving in the Pacific Ocean off the coast of Mexico.

"I was in about forty feet of water, alone. I knew I should not have gone alone, but I was very competent, and just took a chance; there was not much current, and the water was so warm and clear and enticing. But when I got a cramp, I realized at once how foolish I was. I was not very alarmed, but was completely doubled up with stomach cramp. I tried to remove my weight belt, but I was so doubled up I could not get to the catch. I was sinking, and began to feel more frightened, unable to move. I could see my watch, and knew that there was only a little more time on the tank before I would be finished with breathing! I tried to massage my abdomen. I wasn't wearing a wet suit, but couldn't straighten out and couldn't get to the cramped muscles with my hands.

"I thought, 'I can't go like this! I have things to do!' I just couldn't die anonymously this way, with no one to even know what happened to me. I called out in my mind, 'Somebody, something, help me!' "

"Did you really think 'something' as well as 'somebody'?" I asked.

"Yes, I did. I thought of just some vague power coming

to aid me as much as some person. I felt that if there is such a thing as ESP I must try it. So I said, 'Somebody, something, help me.' I was really trying to project my thoughts.

"But I was not prepared for what happened. I had about ten more minutes of oxygen, and was still sinking. Suddenly I felt a prodding from behind me under the armpit. I thought, 'Oh no, sharks!' I felt real terror and despair. But my arm was being lifted forcibly. Around into my field of vision came an eye — the most marvelous eye I could ever imagine. I swear it was smiling. It was the eye of a big dolphin. Looking into that eye, I knew I was safe.

"It moved farther forward, nudging under, and hooked its dorsal fin under my armpit with my arm over its back. I relaxed, hugging it, flooded with relief. I felt that the animal was *conveying* security to me, that it was healing me as well as lifting me toward the surface. My stomach cramp went away as we ascended, and I relaxed with security, but I felt very strongly that it healed me too.

"At the surface, it drew me all the way in to shore. It took me in to water so shallow that I began to be concerned for it, that it would be beached, and I pushed it back a little deeper, where it waited, watching me, I guess to see if I was all right.

"It felt like a new lifetime. When I took off the weightbelt and oxygen, I just took everything off, and went naked back into the ocean to the dolphin. I felt so light and free and alive, and just wanted to play in the sun and the water, in all that freedom. The dolphin took me back out, and played around in the water with me. I noticed that there were a whole lot of dolphins there, farther out. It looked like a hundred of them! It seemed as if they were waiting for this big one. And there were just two others near by, watching us play, but not quite joining in. I felt they were playing with us in spirit. Then my dolphin took me for a ride on its back, with me sitting up like riding a horse, holding on to its dorsal fin. It went so fast that the water rose up to my chin, but never higher, as if it knew just how fast it could go and not drown me.

After a while it brought me back to shore. I was very tired then, almost collapsing, and he made sure I was safe in the shallowest water. Then he turned sideways with one eye looking into mine. We stayed that way for what seemed like a very long time, timeless I guess, in a trance almost, with personal thoughts of the past going through my mind. Then he made just one sound, and went out to join the others, and all of them left."

There has to be a long silence after a story like that.

Then he told me that his life had been affected in subtle ways ever since. "It was basically a spiritual experience. There were subtle changes in me. Subliminal almost. I looked at things with a different perspective." We agreed that it is very difficult to put into words the effect of being exposed to what we might call dolphin consciousness. He spoke of a built-in "governor of truth" that he feels he now has in his life and in his actions. "The dolphin has that, and once you are exposed to that . . . I don't think you can ever . . . it's so hard to express . . . . *You can't ever not know when you are being false.*"

Whatever it is, many of us feel it.

This story is almost a model for what many people dream of as an adventure with a dolphin . . . to need help of some kind in the sea (maybe not being in *that* much danger!), to be rescued by a benevolent and loving animal with an element of almost mysticism in it, then to play. And the crowning event, to be taken for a ride on its back. An adventure with a lot of drama, with fear resolving into security, and love and play. With a lot *happening,* and most especially, getting to ride on the dolphin's back.

Many people ask me eagerly if the dolphins at Monkey Mia will let us ride on their backs. No, they never have done that. Oh . . . disappointment. Sometimes there is almost a sense of: Why bother with a dolphin that won't take you for a ride? I am not sure what is so special about that, but this attitude seems almost universal.

No, these dolphins do not provide that much drama. And they do not take us for rides. But they do provide the other element of Joe's story, that which is so difficult to describe. We talked about the limitations of words. One trouble with words is that they "de-fine," they "set the limits of." "De," down, "fine," finish. There is something about the experience with the dolphins that is just the opposite, that opens our experience rather than closing it. Language so often seems to have that effect of finishing.

Have you ever noticed how the process of describing a dream somehow closes it off, so that the aspects of the dream that you could not describe are somehow lost? (And the best part is that part you were not able to articulate!) The whole spirit, meaning and value of the dream is de-minished by the telling. And then often what we *remember* all the rest of our lives is what we said (or wrote) about the dream, rather than the experience of it, which got lost in the telling. (I have not found it helpful to write my dreams, as many urge us to do, but do find it of great value to close my eyes and relive the dream, avoiding as much as possible getting into language.)

All this says something about the inadequacy of lan-guage. Also, I wonder if a shift into the other brain hemis-phere is involved. We "know" the dream in our whole-knowing (right) side, but when we try to tell about it, that has to take place in the verbal, reasoning (left) side. When we shift sides we lose a bit.

Our "happening" experiences, such as an adventure of riding on a dolphin's back, are easy to describe in language (this happened and then I did this and he did that). But our experience of "knowing" a dolphin is in a different realm; it is not easy to tell about, and is somewhat diminished by an attempt to put it into language. Our experience of knowing a dear human friend is similar. We cannot de-scribe adequately what it means to us, so we rely on drawing upon the listener's own experience with a friend to know what we mean.

Meeting a "dear friend", one with whom we feel a strong rapport, *in the shape of a dolphin* is something of a shock, so we are startled into a greater awareness of that

intimate quality of the experience that is so deeply stirring: being so exposed, so truly recognized and understood, and finding that to be all right. To some degree, perhaps, we would like to avoid facing into this deep knowingness. So we want something to happen, to distract our awareness.

In this book about the dolphins at Monkey Mia there is not much plot. Not so very much happens at that beach. But we do get to know dolphins there. If we are ready to allow ourselves to have this knowingness, we can find it there.

May you, dear reader, find dolphin friends in your own life, whether you wade into the sea to meet them, or find them among the humans you meet — friends who live in openness and harmony and grace, who have a deep consciousness and respect for the natural world around them, who understand and enjoy the great value of play, who perceive your inner-most nature and love you for it, and who know . . .

Postlogue

As this book goes to press in March of 1981, the seasons have taken another turn, and the dolphins have come back for their daily visits at the beach. Wilf Mason wrote me that Nick one day insisted on being given a thorough petting, rubbing his head against Wilf's knee until Wilf tickled him under the chin, under the flippers, and all around his belly and back.

The Dolphin Welfare Foundation has been formed in Denham, with a group of 25 local persons as charter members — a substantial number for the tiny community of Denham. This author has pledged to donate a share of the royalties from *The Dolphins' Gift* to this Australian foundation to help provide a warden for the beach at Monkey Mia. The warden's task is to watch over the dolphins as they come to be touched by humans, and to talk with the people, explaining some facts about dolphins generally and these dolphins in particular. Wilf himself will be this warden, with a salary then so that he can employ someone to do the camp chores, freeing him to watch over the dolphins. Readers who wish to donate to this foundation may do so by sending a check (U.S. dollars) to:

> The Dolphin Welfare Foundation
> Monkey Mia Caravan Park
> P.O. Denham
> W. A. 6537
> Australia

A letter came from Brad Jeffrey, the boy on the back cover of this book, and this is what he said:

The Dolphins

It all started when we left the cold wet winter
of Manjimup to go to the warmth of Shark Bay

approximately 700 miles north of Manjimup. When we got there one of the station hands at Nanga Station said that there were some dolphins at Monkey Mia so we asked Nan to take us and she said yes. When we got there the dolphins were not there but in a matter of minutes they came, seven of them. As soon as I saw them I plunged into the water. The first dolphin came to me and talked in its own dolphin language, then I nodded my head and the dolphin nodded his, then he flew off and got all his friends to circle me, then they flipped their tails and I got wet. Then they flew off into the deep water and started to play. Then they came back. A fisherman gave me a fish to feed them with. I found my dolphin friend and gave the fish to him. Then Nan said we had to go home so we jumped in the car and went back to Nanga. Our adventure with the dolphins was over.

What else has happened at Monkey Mia? The dolphin I observed as B.B.'s friend has begun to come in to be touched ... as I'm sure all of you knew he would. The Mason's daughter Sally had a wedding there. Little Joy Dolphin was a year old in December, and has doubled in size, but has not yet come to be touched. Life goes on for both dolphins and humans in that languid place by the sea.

Cast of Characters

In order of appearance

Old Charley — who rounded up bait fish for the humans for several years in the 1950s and 60s. Not certain if male or female.

Old Speckledy Belly — toothless and wrinkled-mouth dolphin who allowed small children to be placed on her back in the 1970s. She had brown freckles on her belly. Not certain if male or female.

Beautiful — an elegant pale grey mother dolphin who came to take fish from the hand, and brought her suckling calf almost daily to play at the beach the Masons' first year (Dec. 1975). Comes intermittently in 1980.

B.B. — Beautiful's "baby," now a big heavy adolescent, known to many visitors as the dolphin who seems to "tell me something." Comes intermittently in 1980.

Holey-fin — mother dolphin with a suckling calf in early 1976, who comes daily to be petted and take fish. Brought in another new baby at the end of 1979.

Nick — calf of Holey-fin, born probably Dec. 1975, at the time of the Masons' arrival. Brought daily by mother, and now in 1980 is the most regular visitor of all the dolphins, most actively seeking human physical contact. Most show-off performer.

Crooked-fin — adult dolphin who took fish from hand when Masons first came in late 1975. Brought in new calf the following year. Visits almost daily.

Puck — calf of Crooked-fin, born probably Dec. 1976 or Jan. 1977. Brought regularly by mother for years, and now comes almost daily with or without mother.

Joy — Holey-fin's new baby brought in on Dec. 30, 1979.

Snubnose — dolphin new in 1980 who comes to Wilf Mason to take fish.

Rags —

Notch —   adult dolphins who come intermittently in 1980 but who stay at least four or five meters out.

Sickle —

B.B.'s Friend — new visitor in 1980, who swims close with B.B. and/or other dolphins, but stays at least two meters from humans.

Acknowledgements

Thanks are due to many friends who aided and encouraged the writing of this book. First thanks go to Wilf and Hazel Mason who made me so welcome at their beach where the dolphins come to meet us, and who patiently answered all my questions. Appreciation is due also to the many children and adults who shared with me their observations and emotions about the dolphins there, for their stories greatly increase the personal quality of this book.

Next I thank Mark Allen of Whatever Publishing for his unfailing support through the many trying weeks of combing through words, words, words. Without his encouragement this book would have been forgotten halfway through the first draft! Now, here he is, still cheering me on as we come into the last lap.

Next I thank the friends who gave me a place to live as I wrote. One of those interesting coincidences that bemuse me now and then through life came up when I first decided to write the book. My friends the Fraziers were going to Europe for several months and offered me their house. Since it is a pleasant house in Stockton, where I don't know anyone, I realized it would be a perfect place to write without distractions, so I accepted, and began the book. By the time they returned it was two-thirds done, and I was hooked on the project. Now the name of this woman, who has been my dear friend for twenty-five years, is Delphine! I had always thought of her name in association with the flower, delphinium, but suddenly I saw it in a new way. She says she always associated her name unpleasantly with dolphins because she saw them as plump in the middle, but knowing her house was being used to write a dolphin book made her conscious of books all over Europe in several languages about the great intelligence and charm of dolphins, so she feels better about it now. Any-

way, many thanks to Delphine and Tom Frazier for providing the place for the book to be started.

After that I stayed in Sacramento at the home of my very dear friend, Win Mitchel, and wrote the last of the first draft there. She was the first person to read the book, and gave me much kind encouragement. Thank you, Win.

I want to thank Paul Clemens who edited the book. His suggestions were most helpful, although he worked under a severe time pressure. Again there is an interesting co-incidence. Mark Allen had told me he wanted his old friend Paul to do the editing, as he had done such a good edit of Mark's last book. So I set out to drive to the mountains to deliver the manuscript to Paul at his place of work. Mark gave me the address. He works at the Blue Dolphin Press! Obviously this was a great place to get my book edited.

I am very grateful to Stan and Ken Minasian at the Marine Mammal Fund who gave me much friendly help and advice, expecially in preparing prints from my slides to illustrate this book, as well as encouraging me to forge ahead. And thanks to the people I met who told me of their own experiences with dolphins in other places, for these touching stories broaden the perspective of this book.

In the last days of the book preparation, it was a great boost to my energy to work with my old friend, David Fairchild, who so enthusiastically prepared the sketches. And with Jim Konwinski who prepared the photographic prints.

Many thanks to Katherine Dieter for her sweet patience in doing the typesetting.

Last of all, of course, we must all thank my dolphin friends: Holey-fin, Nick, Puck, Crooked-fin, B.B., little Joy, Beautiful, Snub-nose, Sickle-fin, Rags, Notch, and all you other dear creatures who inspired this book. May this publication introduce you and your fellows throughout the world to many new human friends who will learn to love you as I do. Thank you for the gift of your friendship and understanding, your joy and your grace.

Bibliography

Boone, J. Allen. *Kinship with All Life.* New York: Harpen & Row, 1954.

Benchley, Peter. "A Strange Ride in the Deep," *National Geographic,* February, 1981.

Branowsky, Jacob. *The Ascent of Man.* Boston: Little, Brown, 1975.

Brown, Robin. *The Lure of the Dolphin.* New York: Avon Books, 1979.

Coldwell, David and Melba. *The World of the Bottlenosed Dolphin.* Philadelphia: J.B. Lippincott, 1972.

Cousteau, Jacques-Yves and Diole, Philippe. *Dolphins.* New York: A and W Publishers, 1975.

Dark, Eleanor. *The Timeless Land.* Melbourne: Fontana Books, 1973.

Dobbs, Harold. *Follow a Wild Dolphin.* London: Fontana, 1979.

Fichtelius, K. and Sjolander, S. *Smarter than Man?* New York: BAallantine Books, 1974.

Gaskin, D.E. *Whales, Dolphins and Seals.* New York: St. Martin's Press, 1972.

Herbert, Xavier. *Capricornia.* Sydney: Angus & Robertson, 1979.

Kroeber, Theodora. *Ishi, Last of His Tribe.* New York: Bantam Books, 1980.

Lilly, John C. *Man and Dolphin.* New York: Doubleday, 1967.

Lineham, Edward J. "The Trouble with Dolphins," *National Geographic,* April 1979. Vol. 155, No. 4.

McIntyre, Joan. _Mind in the Waters._ San Francisco: Sierra Club Books, 1974.

Minasian, Kenneth. _Dolphins._ San Francisco: Marine Mammal Fund, 1980.

Norris, Kenneth. _Whales, Dolphins and Porpoises._ Berkeley: Univ. California Press, 1966.

Robson, Frank. _Thinking Dolphins, Talking Whales._ Wellington: A.H. & A.W. Reed, Ltd., 1976.

Sagan, Carl. _The Cosmic Connection._ New York: Dell Publishing, 1973.

Sagan, Carl. _Cosmos._ New York: Random House, 1980.

Watson, Lyall. _Super Nature._ Garden City, N.Y.: Anchor Press, 1973.

Photo Credits:
p. 54: *Dolphin* film
p. 174, 238: Dean Campbell
p. 177: Bonnie Dankert
p. 186: New Games
p. 187: Interspecies Communication
All other photos by Elizabeth Gawain

Index

256

About the Author

Elizabeth Gawain is a woman of diverse talents and interests. An urban planner for 25 years, she retired from her career at the age of 54 to pursue her interest in meditation and eastern philosophy. She traveled extensively in Asia, Africa, Europe, Australia and New Zealand for several years, studying and teaching yoga. In 1978 she authored a book on yoga for pregnant women, titled *Yoga with the Unborn*.

During her travels she became deeply interested in dolphins. Her profound personal experiences with these fascinating creatures in their natural environment is chronicled in *The Dolphins' Gift*. Currently living in the San Francisco Bay Area, she travels and lectures widely. Known to her students, friends and family as "Chi-uh," she has one daughter, Shakti Gawain, author of the popular book, *Creative Visualization*.